*The Long Arc of Justice*

# The Long Arc of Justice

*Lesbian and Gay Marriage, Equality, and Rights*

Richard D. Mohr

COLUMBIA UNIVERSITY PRESS    NEW YORK

Columbia University Press
*Publishers Since 1893*
New York   Chichester, West Sussex

This book is a revised version of *A More Perfect
Union: Why Straight America Must Stand Up for Gay
Rights*, published by Beacon Press in 1994.

Library of Congress Cataloging-in-Publication Data

Mohr, Richard D.
   The long arc of justice : lesbian and gay marriage,
equality, and rights /Richard D. Mohr
        p. cm.
   Rev. ed. of: A more perfect union, © 1994
ISBN 0–231–13520–3 (cloth : alk. paper)
ISBN 0–231–50944–8 (e-book)
1. Gays—United States. 2. Gay rights—United States.
3. Same-sex marriage—United States.
I. Mohr, Richard D. More perfect union. II Title.

HQ76.3.USM642   2005
323.3'264'0973—dc22                    2004059318

Columbia University Press books are printed on
permanent and durable acid-free paper.
Printed in the United States of America
c 10 9 8 7 6 5 4 3 2 1

*for Robert W. Switzer,*
*whose heartbeat is my peace*

# Contents

*The Long Arc of Justice*

# Introduction

## A Taboo's End

The moral arc of the universe is long, but it bends towards justice.
—Theodore Parker, American theologian, scholar, and social reformer (1810–1860)

The State cannot demean [homosexuals'] existence or control their destiny.
—U.S. Supreme Court Justice Anthony Kennedy, *Lawrence v. Texas* (2003)

The town I live in is girded by cornfields and good ol' boys. It's nowhere near large enough to support a gay pride parade the last weekend of June, when cities across America commemorate with parades the so-called Stonewall Riots that launched the modern lesbian and gay rights movement in 1969. The town's gay men and lesbians do something at once more radical and more ordinary than that. We have a gay contingent in the town's all-American Fourth of July Parade. The parade draws in crowds from all over the county and much of the rest of east-central Illinois. Last year, as a purple parade banner streamed by the crowds reading "Lesbian and Gay Pride," I saw a little girl, maybe five, lean over to her father and ask, "Daddy, what does *pride* mean?" Apparently she knew what lesbian and gay meant.

This little, local epiphany makes me believe that gay men, lesbians, and our allies are ultimately going to win justice and that we may begin to expect that the course along the moral arc of the universe to justice, though long, is now not that long for lesbians and gay men. We can, at least, now see what the contours of justice for gay men and lesbians look like and where it lies. Still, no one should conclude that the segment of the arc that remains to be traversed will be a simple glide path. In February 2004, the president of the United States called for a constitutional amendment barring lesbian and gay marriages.[1] The call shows there is abiding force in Patrick Buchanan's battle cry, delivered to the 1992 Republican National Convention, that America is in the midst of a cultural war, a war for the hearts and minds—the soul—of the nation, a war over the system of ideas and values by which America defines itself to itself.

The nation's current struggle with lesbian and gay issues is a central battle, possibly *the* central battle in this war over culture. Lesbians and gay men, at least for much of the recent past, have served in the culture's mind as its paradigm of deviance, its exemplar of degeneracy. For instance, it used to be you could tell who the bad guy was in a movie because he wore a black hat. But consider the movies of the 1990s. There the bad guy was simply coded as gay—as in Mel Gibson's *Braveheart*, Oliver Stone's *J.F.K.*, and Jonathan Demme's *Silence of the Lambs*. In the culture's mind, gayness has served as evil made concrete and given life. In some movies, gay men and lesbians could serve as such an intense symbol of evil that their presence relieved moral doubts that we might have had about the movies' heroes—as in David Lean's *Lawrence of Arabia* (1962), where the sadistic gay bey's torturing of Lawrence relieves Lawrence's murderous, vaguely genocidal impulse, "No prisoners!" In Terence Young's *From Russia with Love* (1963), Colonel Klebb's sado-lesbianism relieves Bond's philandering, and in David Lynch's *Dune* (1984), a child molester who literally rips the hearts out of little boys relieves the movie's messianic, vaguely racist, ethic.

So there is a distinct possibility that it will be through America's engagement with lesbian and gay issues that the nation will decide whether it is fundamentally committed to the general values of liberty and equality, which permit and enable individuals to lead their lives by their own lights and with equal dignity, or whether the nation is committed to some specific vision of what constitutes proper living—be it Leftist or Rightist, populist or elitist, secular or religious, but which in any case the nation is willing to impose upon everyone.

* * *

On the broad cultural front, though, gays and lesbians are making rapid progress. Indeed, I suggest that America has passed a crucial turning point on gay issues and is undergoing important structural changes that bode well for the long haul. It is now at least acceptable to inquire about these issues in public discussion. The taboo blanketing talk of lesbians and gay men has all but collapsed. Culturally considered, gays and lesbians are now part of the social landscape, part of human diversity.

The clearest indicator of this shift can be found in the mass media. Certainly movies have changed: in Sam Mendes's *American Beauty*, which won the Academy Award for Best Picture of 1999, the only decent, sane, productive characters are the gay male "couple next door."

As late as 1987, the nation's newspaper of record, the *New York Times*, refused to print the word "gay," but now it carries more gay news than the national gay news magazine the *Advocate*.[2] In August 2003, the *New York Times* began running lesbian and gay wedding announcements from marriages taking place in Canada. In February 2004, the *New York Times* published its first gay wedding announcement for a marriage ceremony that took place in the United States, and in doing so gave its imprimatur to the county-approved, but state-contested, weddings being conducted at San Francisco City Hall.[3] These changes caused a wave of such announcements to begin appearing in other major urban dailies across the nation.[4] And there wasn't a newspaper in the country that failed to run stories and pictures of the first round of American lesbian and gay weddings as they blossomed in a joyous confusion across the country from San Francisco, California, and Portland, Oregon to New Paltz, New York, and all of Massachusetts, welcoming the spring of 2004.

And consider our national pastime, television: in 1996, 32 million Americans watched the lesbian characters Susan and Carol get married on the NBC comedy *Friends*. The next year, 42 million watched Ellen Degeneres's coming out episode. More recently, gays and lesbians have shifted from episodic to full-time evening fare with *Will and Grace*,

*Queer as Folk, Queer Eye for the Straight Guy,* and *The L Word.* Children can now read a nationally syndicated comic strip with a gay male character and even see movie idols and rock stars of the same sex smooching on network television.

A barometric change can also be seen in the mainstream press's reportage of statements about gay men and lesbians. In the summer of 1998, when U.S. Senate majority leader Trent Lott analogized gays to alcoholics and kleptomaniacs, the mainstream press acted as though he had told a racist joke.[5] Even the conservative mainstream press, like *U.S. News & World Report,* editorialized against him.[6] Only three years earlier, when U.S. House speaker Newt Gingrich had drawn similar analogies, they were reported as respectable, if wrong.[7]

A sign that gay men and lesbians are beginning to be thought of as attractive to the nation, or at least as having a transferable glamour, is their recent appearances in mainstream advertising. In its ads for the 2000 Olympic games, John Hancock Financial Services featured a lesbian family. Other national advertising campaigns aimed at mainstream audiences as well have featured gay characters—those for American Express, Absolut Vodka, Subaru, United Airlines, and IKEA Furniture. By 2004, national advertising campaigns for Audi/Volkswagen, General Motors, Target, Cartier, Marshall Field's, Smirnoff's, Chili's restaurants, and Wrigley gums were using gay and lesbian celebrities whose sexual orientation is a significant part of their public personas to pitch their products to straight audiences as urban, edgy, and "now."[8] In the June 6, 2004, *New York Times Magazine,* Grand Marnier ran a full-page ad that consisted of just a small image of its liqueur bottle below a large sans sarif text: "Your sister is finally getting remarried. Her fiancée's name is Jill. The conversation is waiting. Go there."

The importance of lifting the taboo from gay speech, gay issues, and gay lives is enormous. It means that gay or lesbian children will never again have to go through the horror of wondering, "Am I the only one?" Lesbians and gay men can see ourselves as having a place in society, rather than see society putting us "in our place."

The collapse of the taboo will also have—is having—a significant effect on the public lives of many nongay people. On gay issues, people are greatly affected in their opinions by how they think other people will perceive them. Not surprisingly so, for taboos encourage, indeed enforce, the aping of opinions from one person to the next, causing them to circulate independent of critical assessment and authentic feeling. The result is that many nongay people feel socially required to be gay-fearing or gay-hating, even when they are not homophobic by personal inclination. Many people do not on their own feel hostile to gays, but feel compelled to go along with the rituals that degrade and silence gay life, lest they themselves be viewed as morally suspect.

As taboos over talking about gay men and lesbians break down, so too will the echoes and apings that have maintained so many of the social forces directed against gays. Nongay people will be able to express in public contexts their own real feelings. Openly gay U.S. representative Barney Frank has perceptively noted that now "most Americans are less homophobic than they think they are supposed to be."[9] This fortuitous and surprising gap provides great opportunity to those working toward justice for lesbians and gay men.

Further, with the ending of the taboo, antigay forces can no longer automatically count on visceral responses of revulsion to carry the day for them. This change, in turn, has several important corollary effects. First, with the collapse of the taboo, it is increasingly difficult for society to maintain the rituals that demonize gay men and lesbians. Rituals of taboo, notably rituals of the form "don't ask, don't tell," create an eerie supernatural realm unspeakably beyond the pale and then populate it with ghouls and monsters.

Whenever President Bush has spoken about gay marriage, he has managed to do so without actually mentioning "gays" or even "homosexuals." Rather he speaks of "the most fundamental institution of civilization" and then of something that goes unnamed but which assaults it, thus casting gay men and lesbians out there with the ghouls and monsters, even as he says we should all be civil in our discourse on this issue.

With the taboo's collapse, lesbians and gay men, in society's eye, are becoming less like ghouls and monsters and more like hippies and Mormons—or in a metaphor favored by the Right, like alcoholics. Maybe not something nice, maybe something odd, something one might not choose for oneself, but gays are no longer something monstrous, repulsive, unthinkably abject. Though certainly not an ideal attainment, this state of affairs does mark major cultural change.

Second, note that it's okay to know and be around alcoholics and Mormons—and now even to know and be around gay folk. Without demonization, it's hard, perhaps impossible, to think of homosexuality as a contagious disease, one that spreads itself to the pure and innocent by mere proximity. This change of concept will eventually, perhaps already has started to, erode the stereotype of the gay man as child molester and, more generally, as sexual predator. And this change has already markedly lessened for straight folk both fear *of* association and guilt *by* association. For really the first time it is now possible for gays to have straight allies, people who cannot instantly and effectively be tarred and dismissed with the slur "queer lover."

Finally, the collapse of the taboo and of its visceral effects means that antigay forces now have to argue for and give rational accounts of their positions. And the good news here is that the arguments are all on the side of gays. For the ground rules of reasoned discourse—commitments to honesty, consistency, openness, and fair play—make it inherently a force for liberalism.

America is on the verge of treating gay men and lesbians as analogous to a complex religious or ethnic minority, and in turn is playing out the consequences of this view in social policy.

Conservatives sense and fear the cultural shift under way. They seem tacitly to recognize that to win the cultural wars they must shore up the deeply fractured taboo. Just look where conservatives are investing their energies. They are *not* trying to "punish the sin." When, in June 2003, the U.S. Supreme Court, in a case called *Lawrence v. Texas*, knocked down sodomy laws across the country, hardly anyone on the political Right tried defending the substance of sodomy laws.[10] Instead the Right complained about "activist judges." No one called for a constitutional amendment to make sodomy illegal in America again. Rather than trying to punish the sin, conservatives want to get "the sinner" to shut up. Thus they have chiefly focused on *representations* of gay and lesbian life. They target museum exhibitions, the funding of the arts, school curricula, public television, lesbian and gay books, and the *presence* of gays in parades, the military, the Boy Scouts, and the like. And admittedly these efforts have for the most part been successful at least in their narrow, legal, and governmental aims.

But however successful as politics, the conservatives' antigay strategies necessarily trip over themselves as a cultural project. For the more the Right has to talk about things gay, the more the taboo collapses. For example, in 2000, the Supreme Court, with its so-called activist judges, handed a big victory to the Right by giving the Boy Scouts a First Amendment free speech right to discriminate against gays even in the face of state civil rights laws barring such discrimination.[11] But the social fallout from the case has been a financial and pubic relations disaster for the Scouts, as cities, businesses, and charities have withdrawn support from the "moral straight."[12] The Right won this legal war only to lose the cultural peace.

Or ponder, for a second, the phrase "gay marriage." It used to sound to the American ear not just like an oxymoron (say, "a cruel kindness" or "an honest thief"), but a flat-out self-contradiction (say, "a round square" or "a female bachelor"), something that is a logical impossibility, a phrase that was false by the very meaning of its terms, quite independent of any reference to facts. But with all the talk of "gay marriage" generated by the Right, the phrase now sounds about as un-shocking as the phrase "gay couples." Here linguistic reform has helped call into being a real-world possibility. Thanks to the Right's yammering, America, like the White Queen in *Alice in Wonderland*, is believing six impossible things before breakfast.

The new opportunity for reasoned discourse on gay issues raises the question, though: "Now that we can talk, what should we be saying?" Especially for nongay people, the long night of socially enforced silence on gay issues has left a significant void in social thinking.

When talk does turn to gay issues and lives, the results can be quite good. Consider the Supreme Court's 2003 *Lawrence v. Texas* decision, which reversed its much-maligned 1986 decision *Bowers v. Hardwick*.[13] The *Hardwick* decision, which had upheld gay-specific sodomy laws against privacy challenges, was terse, almost summary in its conclusion, and discussed no gay issues. By contrast, more than half of the relatively long *Lawrence* decision is devoted to a discussion of the history of lesbians and gay men in America. At least in one respect, the result was quite stunning. The court didn't simply reverse *Bowers*—that would not have been too unusual, since the Court, on average, reverses itself two or three times a year—but in *Lawrence* the Court also claimed that the earlier case was wrongly decided to begin with. This is extraordinary. Usually the court will reverse a past decision saying that legal doctrines have changed since the case was decided, or that the exceptions have now swallowed the rule, or that developments in one area of the law suggest change in another, or some such move, but rarely, if ever, does the court say flat out that it was wrong in an earlier decision: "*Bowers* was not correct when it was decided, and it is not correct today." The Court's usual phraseology for reversing past cases—*Brown v. Board of Education* reversing *Plessy v. Ferguson,* for instance—is the gingerly "to the extent that the language of case $x$ is inconsistent with our current opinion, it is no longer valid." Such is the transformative power of actually looking at the content of gay and lesbian issues.[14]

In this book I hope to provide a similar reformation in thought across the central issues of lesbian and gay social policy. The book is intended as a handshake of greeting from gay experience to the hearts and minds of mainstream America. By drawing attention to that which is particular about gay and lesbian experience and applying to that experience moral precepts and arguments that Americans as a people have worked through in other areas of national life, the book aims at filling the gaps and enhancing the quality of argumentation in society's thinking on policy issues affecting America's lesbian and gay citizens.

The book is a work of applied ethics. This area of philosophy has been particularly active from the early 1970s to the present. One might date its institutionalization to the founding of the academic journal *Philosophy and Public Affairs* in 1971. Philosophical work in general and this project in particular are centrally concerned with the analysis of arguments, the disambiguating of terms, and the clarification of definitions. So, for instance, key to my chapter on marriage is an analysis of various definitions of marriage, criticizing most, but finding one that actually fits the nation's considered moral and legal experience. The chapter on equality disambiguates several understandings of what equality is, in order to address the important normative and policy question of whether lesbians and gay men form a minority, in a moral sense, on a conceptual par with groups that the country has already given enhanced constitutional and legislated protections (blacks, women, religious groups, the disabled, and others). Philosophy also looks for links between concepts and between disciplines. So the first chapter centrally deals with what stereotypes are, and then the fourth chapter discusses the role that acknowledging the widespread presence of stereotypes in society plays in justifying the placement of constitutional limits on democratic policy-making. This intellectual task is not the sort of thing either a sociologist or legal scholar would likely do, but it links these two fields. The book is not an empirical project, but teases out the normative consequences of empirical studies. So, for instance, whether homosexuality is genetically determined is a question for science. What are the normative consequences of homosexuality's turning out to be genetically determined (or not), that's a question for philosophy. (I address it glancingly in chapter 1 and substantively in chapter 4.)

Taking long-established intellectual equipment into new territory will not be as hopeless as starting a polar expedition equipped only with summer clothing and maps of the Italian lakes, but neither will it be a simple walk around the block. It will, I hope, be an adventure, perhaps one of personal discovery and transformation. For those already committed to working for gays' and lesbians' justice, the book should provide argumentative resources and perhaps a strengthened will for the debates and struggles that lie ahead. For those who are uncertain about what is right for their lesbian and gay fellow citizens, hopefully the book will provide ideas about, and an enhanced sense of, justice, and perhaps even cause a turn of heart. For everybody, including lesbians and gay men ourselves, there is still work to be done in getting emotions and sentiments up to the level where the mind is already leading the way on issues of justice. I hope the prose of the book will help with this rise.

Since applied philosophy analyzes and evaluates moral and ethical arguments, it draws normative conclusions and suggests public policies. This book addresses gay social policy across a wide spectrum of human behaviors and relations. Its content moves across the human spectrum from the intimate to the impersonal, the individual to the social, the private to the political, the material to the symbolic. The first chapter, "Lesbian and Gay Basics: Some Questions, Facts, and Values," clears the ground for the constructive dimensions of the project by addressing the nature of prejudices against lesbians and gay men. The chapter looks at the nature of stereotypes and of their effect on social thinking, and it assesses the standard moral arguments that have been used to try to keep gay men and lesbians from being taken seriously in the first place.

With these impediments addressed, the book's constructive project begins with two chapters that look at intimacy, in particular at the proper relations between sex, love, privacy, and daily life. The first chapter addresses sexual privacy; the second, gay marriage. In these chapters, I try to give deference to all registers of the soul. Against strong cultural forces to the contrary, I argue that sexuality is a freestanding good, and so I at least try to keep a candle lit for sexual liberation, even while arguing that civil marriage is an institution that the gay and lesbian community can legitimately embrace for those of its members who wish to wed and that legal bars to same-sex marriage are profoundly unjust.

The Supreme Court in *Lawrence* was so concerted in its drive to overturn *Bowers* that it failed to explain adequately why gays', lesbians', or indeed anyone's sexual behavior should be protected by a right to privacy. The Court's privacy analysis is brief and congested. As important: the Court asserted a right of sexual privacy with only the weakest possible force that any right can have—a vanishingly slight one. The weakness of this right, and of the case's arguments, has left lower courts free to act as though *Lawrence* had never been written when they have gone on to address related gay and lesbian issues, like the constitutionality of laws barring adoptions by lesbians and gay men and of sexual-orientation specific "Romeo and Juliet" laws, that is, laws which modify statutory rape penalties when the perpetrator and "victim" are near in age.[15] These laws have been upheld in state and lower federal courts despite *Lawrence*. The right to sexual privacy needs a stronger defense than *Lawrence* gave it, and in the book's second chapter I aim to do exactly that. I defend the right to privacy covering sexual behavior as an important, fundamental right with a force as strong as any constitutional protection. I then go on to argue that given the nature and strength of this right, past and ongoing attempts to address the problem of AIDS through punitive and coercive measures are illegitimate.

In the third chapter I explore the lesbian and gay controversy that whelmed upon the nation's social, religious, and political scene in the winter–spring of 2004—gay marriage. I suggest that we cannot determine whether gay men and lesbians should have access to marriage until we first know what marriage is. Surprisingly little analytical work has addressed definitional issues surrounding marriage. Everyone seems to think that what marriage is is so obvious that no analysis is needed. I argue that the standard legal definition fails along several dimensions as an explanation of what marriage is and that marriage is, at heart, not an invention of the law, though that is a myth which the law itself wants us to believe—that "civil marriage is created through exercise of the state's police power," as Massachusetts's highest court leadenly put it in its November 2003 decision declaring unconstitutional bars to same-sex couples marrying in the Bay State.[16] I argue instead that marriage, in the first instance, is a mode of daily living, a type of connection between persons, one that most closely resembles old-fashioned common law marriages, in which one's primary love relationship is developed in the very household in which one's basic needs are met, indeed through the very means by which one's basic needs are met.

Such a pairing of love and need is not an eternal verity scripted in nature for all to follow. Famously, sixth- and early fifth-century Athens strictly separated intimacy and necessity. The household was the realm of necessity and nothing more. A citizen's wife was a functional creature, not a love object. She managed the household slaves and bore children, and that was that. The citizen himself conducted his passionate love relationships outside the household—with either a series of concubines or a series of lads between the age of puberty and the growth of a stiff beard. There lay love divine.

In the Anglo-American tradition, marriage blends intimacy and need in day-to-day living. Speaking metaphorically, we might say that marriage is an organic amalgam of the divine and the material, of sanctity and necessity. The function of marital law is to support this fragile life form, one in which gay and lesbian couples are as properly full participants as are any other couples.

Throughout the book, I presume that the state may carry out well-motivated projects as long as they do not trench on fundamental rights. It is only within the area of religion—and there perhaps largely for historical reasons—that the Constitution requires the state to be neutral between different styles of living: "Congress shall make no law respecting an establishment of religion." But as long as the state does not weight marriage so heavily that it de facto coerces participation in it, and so long as marriage does not violate the equality rights of single people, then the law is permitted to enhance the prospects of its flourishing. What constitutes an inequitable treatment of a group is addressed in the next chapter.

In the remaining chapters, I address the gay person as a social creature and community member. I examine civil relations, that is, relations conducted between people at arm's length. I explore how people can be fair to each other while conducting activities in the public spheres of the workplace and civic life.

The fourth chapter explores the elusive notion of equality. America's intuitions about equality are neither as strong nor as clear as are its intuitions about liberty. The concept of liberty has been knocking around the nation's central political conscience since the Bill of Rights, equality only since Civil War's end. Imagine how deflationary the peroration of Martin Luther King Jr.'s "I Have a Dream" speech would have been if it had ended: "Equal at last! Equal at last! Thank God Almighty, we are equal at last!" Yet it was chiefly equality, not liberty, that King was after.

Analysis will show that equality is primarily a matter of having equal dignity, not equal opportunity, that equality, at its core, is a principle of nondegradation. Since many American folkways view gays as having a degraded existence, equality is a particularly important value for sorting out gay issues, yet it is on issues of equality that gays have made the least progress to date. Neither the Supreme Court nor any of the thirteen federal circuit courts, for example, has viewed gays as having the same levels of protection against governmental discrimination that blacks, women, and even illegal immigrant children have.[17] The chapter gives reasons for changing this view. Along the way, I explain what is meant by a minority in a moral sense and why civil-union arrangements do not treat lesbian and gay couples equitably, even if they give same-sex couples every single right and benefit that marriage confers on heterosexual couples.

In the fifth chapter I argue for the extension of civil rights laws to gay men and lesbians. These laws would bar discrimination against lesbians and gay men in private sector employment, housing, and public services. They would establish for gay men and lesbians the same rights that the 1964 Civil Rights Act affords blacks, women, and religious minorities. For the longest part of the gay rights movement, it was these rights that were typically referred to when gay men and lesbians used the phrase "gay rights." The press for such rights has now been at least partially eclipsed and perhaps even stalled by the controversies swirling around gay marriage. But the lesbian and gay movement will eventually want to return to the work of making sure such legislation is passed. The chapter provides the argumentative armature for such work.

The final chapter, the sixth, addresses gay and lesbian issues at the point where the individual becomes impersonally fused with the functions of government—becomes the citizen-soldier. I first offer a moral critique of the current military ban on lesbians and gay men—a ban that takes the form "don't ask, don't tell." I then offer a cultural critique of the symbolic significance of the current military ban on gay men in particular. Culturally speaking, the military is one of the chief institutions, perhaps the chief institution, by participation in which America defines full personhood, and in turn it ties that participation to manhood and combat. Only by understanding the military's role in the way Americans define themselves to themselves, especially define and patrol gender identities, can one can begin to understand the workings and full insidiousness of the ban on gays serving their country.

The book's conclusion looks to the future and explores how both the nation's symbolic use of gay issues and the nation's current progress in addressing gay issues suggest that a culturally focused gay politics will have the best likelihood of drawing the country nearer to justice for lesbians and gay men.

* * *

Soon after my little epiphany with the little girl at the Fourth of July parade, my partner of twenty-five years proposed to me—by e-mail. Very postmodern. And very romantic: "Do you think we should do this?" I had been thinking of popping the question myself, but hadn't come up with a clever enough wording yet. Our engagement was set within weeks of the Ontario supreme court's ruling on June 10, 2003, that the province's different-sex-only marriage law violated the Canadian constitution.[18] The ruling made Ontario the first place on Earth where gay American couples could legally wed. We had met in Toronto, the graduate student and the social welfare worker, and began living together there in 1978. So we did not feel like interlopers. Instead the marriage option felt like a right of return. Fearing the opportunity might vanish, we tracked, like eagles, the twists and turns of the Canadian political parties as they responded to the court's ruling. Would the conservatives succeed in getting the government to invoke a special legislative override provision in the Canadian constitution to suspend the Ontario ruling? They did not.[19] Would the federal government pass legislation legalizing same-sex marriage nationwide, as it said it would as part of its announcement that it was not appealing the Ontario ruling to the Canadian Supreme Court. It did not.

Through all of this, we were planning. Rings were scouted and ordered at Tiffany's, menus for the wedding reception and dinner drawn up, reservations booked for the honeymoon suite at a rustic lodge in Quebec, wedding announcements designed and printed: "Rings? Yes. Registries? No. We eloped." Toronto friends would treat us to the wedding night in a suite at the city's 1903 King Edward Hotel. Even without crinoline and lace, there was lots to do.

Beyond the serious emotional, social, and political content of marriage, there were fun bits, ironic bits, bits that only the postmodern era could call into being. In Ontario, marriage licenses are issued by the Province's Ministry of Consumer and Business Services. Are we consumers or are we a business? Better: licenses come—like prisoners or bar-coded food items—with bureaucracy-generated, bureaucracy-ready file numbers. Our license is E253377. So much for romance. Best: in Massachusetts, marriage licenses are issued by the Department of Public Health—as though typhus, syphilis, sewage spills, and, well, heterosexuality were all peas in a pod. So much for the much-vaunted legal sacredness of traditional marriage.

With planning, ironies, and a willing government all in play, we wed November 24, 2003. That Sunday, the *New York Times* ran our announcement, with photograph, in the "Weddings/Celebrations" pages of its *Sunday Styles* section. There we were, a couple of slobs tucked in among the debutantes, captains of industry, and directors of major charities. Not civilly united, not ceremonially committed, not domestically partnered, but married pure and simple. We were the tenth same-sex couple to be announced as married in the *New York Times*.

Our local newspaper refuses to allow the term "partner" or even "companion" to be used in obituaries, but it ran a feature article with us beaming forth from the front page of its weekly lifestyles section. On the day the president called for a constitutional amendment barring gay marriages, the local NBC-TV affiliate led off its six o'clock news by interviewing us. The *St. Louis Post-Dispatch* ran a narrative feature on our daily rituals and routines, "Two Men in a Marriage." The article was saccharine enough to give readers diabetes. But people loved it. Our fifteen minutes stretched to twenty. It felt like we were living history.

Through this unfolding process, responses flowed in from many quarters. All the tidings and wishes were good. During the wedding reception, we received from the chancellor of the university where we both work a floral congratulation that dwarfed the bellhop who delivered the arrangement. Strangers have stopped us on the street to offer congratulations. I heard from high school classmates I couldn't even remember. Our state representative laminated the local newspaper article together with her business card and sent them to us—some things never change. We lead multidimensional lives that put us in contact with many people whose politics we have no occasion to know, but the response was uniform and robust from these people and even from a couple of people I know to be fundamentalists. It wasn't the gift certificates and bottles of champagne that were impressive, it was the authenticity of the response. Put a face on gay marriage and it calls everyone's bluff.

Surprisingly, the response seemed to be stronger from straights than gays—surprising given the number of gay couples who have gotten married the very instant the possibility presented itself. This difference may have resulted from vestigial self-hatred on the part of gays, but I think it more likely the result of nongays simply having so many more ready-to-hand traditions to draw on when addressing the oddnesses that pop up when old ways are transposed onto new turf. In any case, the wedding and its offshoots have made me cautiously optimistic that gays and nongays can move together toward justice, can converge in a united agenda, even in the areas of social policy that seem to be most troubling to mainstream culture. My hope is that this book will help in the convergence.

June 2004
Urbana, Illinois

*Chapter 1*

# Lesbian and Gay Basics:
# Some Questions, Facts, and Values

Over the last decade, gay men and lesbians have begun to make steady progress in getting our issues debated—in the courts, at city hall, in state houses, in Congress, and by the White House. But there remain structural impediments to lesbians and gay men making consistent progress in shepherding our interests across these debates on into public policy, social practice, and law. Ironically, just as the progress that gays have made to date has largely been cultural, so too are the undertows that trip up further progress. These undertows include: the persistence of antigay stereotypes; a belief held by some that discrimination against gays is slight and so not a major social worry; a widespread belief, sometimes religiously based, that gays are somehow immoral, perverse, even willfully perverse; and a fear that changing social policies concerning lesbians and gay men will usher in other, undesirable, possibly cataclysmic changes. This chapter seeks to address these problems and allay these fears.

Increasingly the average American knows someone who is lesbian or gay. In 1985, only one in five Americans claimed to have a friend or acquaintance who was a lesbian or a gay man.[1] In 2004, 40 percent of Americans claimed to have a close friend or family member who was a gay man or lesbian. When the question was expanded to ask after acquaintances as well, 69 percent of Americans claimed to know a lesbian or gay male.[2] This is important progress. Even so, much, perhaps most, of America's experience with gay men and lesbians is not firsthand, but mediated—has cultural rather than personal sources. First among these cultural sources are stereotypes that warp people's perception of lesbians and gay men, and can even swamp or erase the benefits of firsthand experience. For people tend to hold onto stereotypes even when their own circle includes friends who directly contradict the stereotype.

Mainstream media—television first among them—abound in portrayals of gay people (particularly gay men) that reinforce stereotypes rather than undercut them, especially in the absence of any programming that presents a hearty number of ordinary gay people. For example, cultural critics have argued that *Queer as Folk* reinforces the stereotype of gay men as aggressively promiscuous, while *Queer Eye for the Straight Guy* reinforces the stereotype of gay men as flighty ditzes.

To their credit, these two television programs have helped to defang the term "queer" and even launch it into some areas of mainstream circulation with a positive valance. But the shows also may be seen as emblems of the two oddly contradictory stereotypes of gay people that still persist in our culture. On the one hand, gay people are seen as confused about their gender identity: lesbians are females who want to be, or at least look and act like, men—thus, the aspersions *bull dykes* and *diesel dykes*; while gay men are males who want to be, or at least look and act like, women—thus the aspersions *queen, fairy, nance, limp-wrist, nelly, sissy,* and *auntie*. These stereotypes of mismatches between biological sex and socially defined gender roles provide the fodder for ethnic-like jokes, which, though derisive, basically view lesbians and gay men as ridiculous: "How many fags does it take to change a light bulb?" Answer: "Eight—one to replace it and seven to scream 'Faaaaaabulous!'"

The other set of stereotypes casts gays as a pervasive, sinister, conspiratorial threat. The core stereotype here is that of gay people—especially gay men—as sex-crazed maniacs, and very likely child molesters, but in any case vampire-like creatures that aggressively spread around a corruptive contagion. These stereotypes carry with them fears of the very destruction of family and civilization itself. The contradiction between these two images is obvious: something that is essentially ridiculous can hardly have such a staggering and menacing effect. Something must be afoot.

Clarifying the nature of stereotypes can help make sense of this incoherent amalgam. Stereotypes are not simply false generalizations from a skewed sample of cases examined. Admittedly, false generalizing plays some part in the stereotypes society holds about gays and other groups. For instance, most studies before the 1960s were based almost entirely on gay men who were in psychiatric hospitals or prisons, and not surprisingly, these men proved to be of a crazed or criminal cast. Such false generalizations, though, simply confirmed beliefs already held on independent grounds, ones that likely led the investigator to the prison and psychiatric ward to begin with. Evelyn Hooker, who in the late 1950s carried out the first rigorous studies of nonclinical gay men, found that psychiatrists, when presented with case files including all the standard diagnostic psychological profiles—but omitting indications of sexual orientation—were unable to distinguish gay files from nongay ones, even though they believed gay men to be crazy and themselves to be the experts at detecting craziness.[3] These studies proved a profound embarrassment to the psychiatric establishment, which profited throughout the twentieth century by attempting to "cure" allegedly insane gays. Hooker's studies ultimately led the way to the American Psychiatric Association's decision, in 1973, to drop homosexuality from its registry of mental illnesses. Nevertheless, the stereotype of gays as "sick" continues apace in the mind of America. And the American Psychiatric Association still thinks it is acceptable for its members to try to change the sexual orientation of gays who are unhappy about being gay. The APA merely changed the name of the diagnosis to "ego-dystonic homosexuality" and then, in 1994, changed that diagnosis, in turn, to "persistent and marked distress about one's sexual orientation."[4] The disingenuousness of this orientation-neutral reform is clear: through the miracle of political correctness, it seems that the APA would have us believe that there are heterosexuals out there who are so distressed about their sexual orientation that they should pay psychiatrists good money to be converted into happy homosexuals.

False generalizations help maintain stereotypes; they do not form them. As the history of Hooker's discoveries shows, stereotypes have a life beyond facts; their origin lies in a culture's ideology—the general system of beliefs by which it lives—and they are sustained across generations by diverse cultural transmissions, including slang and jokes, which don't even purport to have a scientific basis. Stereotypes, then, are not the products of bad science, but reflections of society's conception of itself.

But these reflections do not just passively sit around in the mind as inert bits of false opinion, in the way, say, dated or inaccurate statements might sit around inert in an old encyclopedia. Rather they have an active role in how a person takes in the world. They are part of the apparatus, lenses, if you will, through which the mind perceives the world. If you look through a lens with a tree painted on it, you see a tree everywhere. If you look through a pink lens, the world is pink. The lens filters out other colors. Stereotypes determine what we take to be "the facts," to be good evidence, sound ideas, even logical arguments. For they screen out any fact, idea, or argument that disagrees with what a person believes already.

Stereotypes can literally cause a person to see things. Consider, for example, the initial round of gay weddings in San Francisco during February 2004. When newly hitched lesbian and gay couples would emerge from city hall, well-wishers in the plaza below would shout hurrahs. A week into these weddings, the Austrian-born governor of California was in town for a state Republican convention. Two days later he reported to NBC's *Meet the Press* on the gay marriages he thought he had seen: "All of a sudden we see riots and we see protest and we see people clashing. The next thing we know is there's injured or there's dead people."[5] The *New York Times* reported of the very same events: "The San Francisco police reported no violence related to the same-sex marriage certificates."[6] The stereotype of gays as destroyers of civilization made the governor see jubilation as civilization destroyed—anarchy. The stereotype caused the governor to project onto experience something he already believed and then use the stereotype-manipulated experience to reinforce beliefs he held already linking gays and anarchy—beliefs he felt so confident about that he would trot them out onto national television.

On this understanding of stereotypes, as culturally implanted lenses with a social agenda in mind, it is easy to see how the main antigay stereotypes operate in society's conception of itself. Stereotypes about gays as gender-confused reinforce powerful gender roles that are still prevalent in American society. These stereotypes condemn the possibility of choosing a social role independent of one's biological sex—a possibility that might threaten many guiding social divisions, both domestic and commercial. Blurred would be the socially sex-linked distinctions between breadwinner and homemaker, boss and secretary, doctor and nurse, protector and protected, even God and his world. The accusations "fag" and "dyke" serve in significant part to keep women in their place and to prevent men from breaking ranks and ceding away theirs.

The stereotypes of gays as destroyers of civilization function to displace (possibly irresolvable) social problems from their actual source to a remote and (society hopes) manageable one. For example, the stereotype of the gay person as child molester functions to give the traditionally defined family unit a false sheen of innocence. It keeps the unit from being examined too closely for incest, child abuse, wife-battering, and the terrorizing of women and children by a father's constant threats. The stereotype teaches that the problems of the family are alien to it, not internal to it.

If this account of stereotypes holds, society has been profoundly immoral. For its treatment of gays is a grand scale rationalization, a moral sleight-of-hand. The problem is not that society's usual standards of evidence and procedure in decision-making have been misapplied to gays. Rather, when it comes to gays, the standards themselves have simply been ruled out of court and disregarded in favor of mechanisms that encourage unexamined fear and hatred.

\* \* \*

Partly because lots of people still suppose they don't personally know any gay people, and partly because of the ongoing effects of stereotypes, society at large is not fully aware of the many ways in which lesbians and gay men are still subject to discrimination. Contributing to this ignorance is the difficulty for gay people, as an invisible minority, even to complain of discrimination, especially workplace discrimination. For if one is gay, to register a complaint would suddenly target oneself as a stigmatized person, and so, especially in the absence of any protection against discrimination, would simply invite more discrimination. So, discrimination against lesbians and gay men, like rape, goes seriously underreported. Even so, known discrimination is widespread.

Annual studies by the National Gay and Lesbian Task Force have consistently found that more than 90 percent of gay men and lesbians have been victims of violence or harassment in some form on the basis of their sexual orientation. Greater than one in five gay men and nearly one in ten lesbians have been punched, hit, or kicked; a quarter of all gays have had objects thrown at them; a third have been chased; a third have been sexually harassed; and nearly one-seventh have been spit on, all just for being perceived to be gay.

The most extreme form of antigay violence is queerbashing—where groups of young men target a person who they suppose is a gay man and beat and kick him unconscious and sometimes to death amid a torrent of taunts and slurs. In July 1999 at Fort Campbell, Kentucky, Pvt. Calvin Glover goaded Pvt. Barry Winchell into a fistfight. Glover lost the fistfight to Winchell, a soldier widely perceived in the barracks to be gay. The next night, a third soldier egged on and taunted Glover to defend his lost manhood—after all what could be more humiliating than to be beaten by a sissy?—and so Glover clubbed Winchell to death with a baseball bat as he slept. Glover got a life sentence, the friend twelve and a half years.[7]

But many queerbashing cases never reach the courts. Those that do are frequently marked by inequitable procedures and results. Judges will describe queerbashers as "just All-American boys." In a particularly disturbing case from the 1980s, a District of Columbia judge handed suspended sentences to queerbashers whose victim had been stalked, beaten, stripped at knife point, slashed, kicked, threatened with castration, and pissed on, because the judge thought the bashers were good boys at heart—they went to a religious prep school.[8] Current-day queerbashing functions somewhat similarly to past lynchings of blacks—to keep a whole stigmatized group in line. As with lynchings, society has routinely averted its eyes, giving its permission or even tacit approval to violence and harassment. These inequitable procedures show that the life and liberty of gays, like those of blacks, count for less than the life and liberty of members of the dominant culture.

There has been some progress on this front over the last decade. Thanks to the nationwide publicity given to the particularly brutal, Crucifixion-invoking murder of Matthew Shepard in Laramie, Wyoming, in October 1998, and to the subsequent trials and convictions of his assailants and their accomplices, queerbashers have had more difficulty mounting successful defenses which argue that their actions were a form of justified self-defense.[9] In such so-called homosexual panic defenses, the killer would simply claim his act was an understandable, automatic response to a sexual overture. It was the victim's fault; he provoked his own death. In the Shepard case, the judge barred the defense team from presenting such a defense, since it turns on and reinforces prejudices against gays.[10] This ruling has set a judicial pattern for the rest of the country.

Still, as long as the stereotype of gays as child molesters lives, many will believe, at least subconsciously, that when gays are attacked, they are just getting what they deserve. And young males can still find "out there" in popular culture lots of support for the violence they direct against gay men. In February 2001, the white rap artist Eminem won three Grammy Awards, including best rap album for his *Marshall Mathers LP*, which had sold 5.2 million copies in just two months after its May 2000 release.[11] Of the record's eighteen tracks, thirteen belittle gay men and lesbians; one portrays gay men as child molesters; one ridicules gay marriage; many include threats of lethal violence against gay men and lesbians ("My words are like a dagger that'll stab you in the head whether you're a fag or les"), often with a side appeal to a "homosexual panic" justification ("You faggots keep eggin me on til I have you at knifepoint"). The tracks culminate in a genocidal fantasy:

"You faggots can vanish to volcanic ash. And re-appear in hell with a can of gas, and a match."

Where young males are violent by government order, gay men and lesbians are also discriminated against. Lesbians and gay men are barred from military service. Until 1993, the bar was a Department of Defense directive that could have been changed by the president or Joint Chiefs of Staff. That year, it became a federal statute, which can now be reversed only if Congress passes a new law or the federal courts declare the ban unconstitutional—something they have shown no inclination to do.

In 1996, Congress passed the so-called Defense of Marriage Act, which prevents the federal government from giving legal recognition to any same-sex marriages and permits states to do the same. By the spring of 2004, thirty-eight states had taken up the federal offer and passed laws barring both in-state same-sex marriages and the recognition of those from out of state. A 1997 report that the Government Accounting Office researched and published in response to a request from the U.S. House Judiciary Committee found 1,049 federal laws that provide benefits, rights, and privileges only to those who are married.[12] By barring gays from military service and from marrying, governments do more than directly withhold rights and benefits from gays; they also set a precedent favoring discrimination in the private sector.

The federal government no longer has a blanket ban on gay employment in the CIA, FBI, National Security Agency, and the State Department—though these agencies continue to defend in the courts a right to discriminate and continue to take sexual orientation into account in making case-by-case hiring decisions.[13] State and local governments regularly fire gay or lesbian teachers, police officers, firefighters, social workers, and anyone who has contact with the public. Further, state licensing laws (though frequently honored only in the breach) officially bar gays from a vast array of occupations and professions—everything from doctors, lawyers, accountants, and nurses to hairdressers, morticians, even used-car dealers. Though gay sexual acts are now constitutionally protected, states still take them as marks of immoral personalities and so as making one unfit for whole swaths of employment opportunities. In its 2003 case *Lawrence v. Texas,* which declared sodomy laws unconstitutional, the Supreme Court punted on a perfect opportunity to block this whole line of discriminatory thinking.[14]

Gays are subject to discrimination in a wide variety of other ways, including private-sector employment, public accommodations, housing, child custody, adoption, and zoning regulations that bar "nonrelated" couples from living together.

Discrimination and the absorption by gay men and lesbians of society's traditional hatred of them interact to impede and, for some, block altogether the ability to create and maintain significant personal relations with loved ones. Every facet of life is affected by discrimination. Only the most compelling reasons could justify it.

\* \* \*

Many people and, as noted, many states think society's treatment of gays is justified because they think gays are immoral. To evaluate this claim, different senses of "moral" must be distinguished. Sometimes "morality" just means the values generally held by members of a society—its mores, norms, and customs. On this understanding, gays are probably not moral: lots of people hate them, and social customs are designed to register widespread disapproval of gays. The problem here is that this sense of morality is merely a descriptive one. On this understanding, every society has a morality—even Nazi society, which had racism and mob rule as central features of its "morality" understood in this sense. What is needed in order to use the notion of morality to praise or condemn behavior is a sense of morality that is prescriptive or normative.

As the Nazi example makes clear, the fact that a lot of people in a society say something is good, even over eons, does not make it so. The rejection of the long history of socially approved and state-enforced slavery is another good example of this principle at work. Slavery would be wrong even if nearly everyone liked it. If the only justification for viewing gays as immoral is that most people dislike or disapprove of them, then consistency and fairness require that one abandon the belief.

Furthermore, recent historical and anthropological research has shown that opinion about gays has been by no means universally negative. It has varied widely even within the larger part of the Christian era and even within the church itself.[15] There are even current societies—most notably in Papua, New Guinea—where compulsory homosexual behavior is integral to the rites of male maturity.[16] Within the last forty years, American society has undergone a grand turnabout from deeply ingrained, near total condemnation to near total acceptance on two emotionally charged "moral" or "family" issues—contraception and divorce. Society holds its current descriptive morality of gays not because it has to, but because it chooses to.

Clearly, popular opinion and custom are not enough to ground moral condemnation of homosexuality. Religious arguments are also frequently used to condemn homosexuality. Such arguments usually proceed along two lines. One claims that the condemnation is a direct revelation of God, usually through the Bible. The other sees condemnation in God's plan as manifested in nature; homosexuality (it is claimed) is "contrary to nature."

One of the more remarkable discoveries of recent gay research is that the Bible may not be as univocal in its condemnation of homosexuality as many have believed. Christ never mentions homosexuality. Recent interpreters of the Old Testament have pointed out that the story of Lot at Sodom is probably intended to condemn inhospitality rather than homosexuality. Further, some of the Old Testament condemnations of homosexuality seem simply to be ways of tarring those of the Israelites' opponents who happen to accept homosexual practices when the Israelites themselves did not. If so, the condemnation is merely a quirk of history and rhetoric rather than a moral precept.

What does seem clear is that those who regularly cite the Bible to condemn an activity like homosexuality do so by selective reading. Do clergy who cite what they take to be condemnations of homosexuality in Leviticus maintain in their lives all the hygienic, dietary, and marital laws of Leviticus? If they cite the story of Lot at Sodom to condemn homosexuality, do they also cite the story of Lot in the cave to condone incestuous rape? It seems then not that the Bible is being used to ground condemnations of homosexuality as much as society's dislike of homosexuality is being used to interpret the Bible.[17]

Even if a consistent portrait of condemnation could be gleaned from the Bible, what social significance should it be given? One of the guiding principles of society, enshrined in the Constitution as a check against government, is that decisions affecting social policy are not made on religious grounds. The Religious Right has been successful in defunding gay safe-sex literature and gay art, and in blocking the introduction of gay materials into school curriculums. If the real ground of the alleged immorality invoked by governments to discriminate against gays is religious (as it seems to be in these cases), then one of the major commitments of our nation is violated. Religious belief is a fine guide around which a person might organize his or her own life, but an awful instrument around which to organize someone else's life.

In the second kind of religious argument, people try to justify society's treatment of lesbians and gay men by saying they are unnatural.[18] Though the accusation of unnaturalness looks whimsical when taken as a general explanation of immorality, it is usually delivered with venom of forethought when applied to homosexuality. It carries a high emotional charge, usually expressing disgust and evincing queasiness. Probably it is nothing but an emotional charge. For people get equally disgusted and queasy at all sorts of things that are perfectly natural and that can hardly be fit subjects for moral condemnation. Two typical examples in current American culture are some people's responses to mothers' breastfeeding in public and to women who do not shave body hair. And nearly everyone thinks the idea of their own parents having sex, especially the sex that had them, is gross, gross, gross. But surely it's both perfectly natural and morally permissible. In like manner, people fling the term "unnatural" against gays in the same breath and with the same force as when they call gays "sick" and "gross." To explain his March 2004 vote in the Georgia House of Representatives for an amendment to the Georgia constitution barring gay marriage, the Rev. Randal Mangham emoted, "I don't appreciate having to explain to my 9-year-old why two big husky guys are kissing."[19] When people have strong emotional reactions, as they do in these cases, without being able to give good reasons for them, they can hardly be thought of as operating morally; more likely they are obsessed and manic.

When "nature" is taken in technical rather than ordinary usages, it also cannot ground a charge of homosexual immorality. When unnatural means "by artifice" or "made by humans," it can be pointed out that virtually everything which is good about life is unnatural in this sense. The chief feature that distinguishes people from other animals is people's very ability to make over the world to meet their needs and desires. Indeed people's well-being depends upon these departures from nature. On this understanding of human nature and the natural, homosexuality is perfectly unobjectionable; it is simply a means by which some people adapt nature to fulfill their need and desires.

Another technical sense of natural is that something is natural and so, good, if it fulfills some function in nature. On this view, homosexuality is unnatural because it violates the function of genitals, which is to make babies. One problem with this view is that lots of bodily parts have lots of functions and just because some one activity can be fulfilled by only one organ (say, the mouth for eating), this activity does not condemn other functions of the organ to immorality (say, the mouth for talking, licking stamps, or blowing bubbles). So the possible use of the genitals to produce children does not, without more, condemn the use of the genitals for other purposes, say, achieving ecstasy and intimacy.

The notion of function seemed like it might ground moral authority, but instead it turns out that moral authority is needed to define "proper function." If God is the moral authority, we are back to square one—holding others accountable to one's own religious beliefs.

Finally, people sometimes attempt to establish the authority for a moral obligation to use bodily parts in a certain fashion simply by claiming that moral laws are natural laws and vice versa. On this account, inanimate objects and plants are good in that they follow natural laws by necessity, animals follow them by instinct, and persons follow them by a rational will. People are special in that they must first discover the laws that govern them. Now, even if a person believes the view—dubious in the post-Newtonian, post-Darwinian world—that natural laws in the usual sense ($e = mc^2$, for instance) have some moral content, it is not at all clear how he or she is to discover the laws in nature that apply to people.

On the one hand, if one looks to people themselves for a model—and looks hard enough—one finds amazing variety, including homosexual relations as a social ideal (as in upper-class sixth-century Athens) and even as socially mandatory (as in some Melanesian initiation rites today). When one looks to people, one is simply unable to strip away the layers of social custom, history, and taboo in order to see what's really there to any degree more specific than that people are the creatures who make over their world and are capable of abstract thought. Or as Hannah Arendt put it, human beings are the creatures whose nature it is to have no nature.[20] That this is so should raise doubts that neutral principles are to be found in human nature that will condemn homosexuality.

On the other hand, if one looks to nature apart from people for models, the possibilities are staggering. Orangutans, genetically our next of kin, live completely solitary lives without social organization of any kind among adults: ought we to "follow nature" and be hermits? There are fish that change sex over their lifetimes: should we all "follow nature" and be transsexuals? There are many species where only two members per generation reproduce: shall we be bees? The search in nature for people's purpose far from finding sure models for action is likely to leave one morally rudderless.

* * *

But (it might be asked) aren't gays willfully the way they are? Social scientists have found that people who believe being gay is something fixed in a person's basic constitution are much more likely to support gay rights than people who think that being gay is something that one can cast off, in the way one could cease being a liar, thief, or Elvis fan. And it is widely conceded that if sexual orientation is something over which an individual—for whatever reason—has virtually no control, then discrimination against gays is presumptively wrong, as it is against racial and ethnic classes. Indeed most of the popular debate on lesbian and gay issues has turned on this very issue. Groups like Parents and Friends of Lesbians and Gays (PFLAG) doggedly believe that being gay is biologically determined, while most fundamentalists believe that being gay is a form of habitual sinning that, like a penchant for sweets or alcohol, can be given up with effort. I give a preliminary

"take" on this issue here and then provide a more nuanced understanding of the problem in chapter 4 ("Equality").

Attempts to answer the question whether or not sexual orientation
is something that is reasonably thought to be within one's own control
usually appeal simply to various claims of the biological or "mental"
sciences. But the ensuing debate over genes, hormones, hypothala-
muses, twins, early childhood development, and the like is as unnecessary as it is currently inconclusive.[21] All that is needed to answer the
question is to look at the actual experience of lesbians and gay men in
recent society and it becomes fairly clear that sexual orientation is not
likely a matter of choice.

On the one hand, the "choice" of the gender of a sexual partner
does not seem to express a trivial desire that might as easily be fulfilled
by a simple substitution of the desired object. Picking the gender of a
sex partner is decidedly dissimilar, that is, to such activities as picking
a flavor of ice cream. If an ice cream parlor is out of one's flavor, one
simply picks another. And if people were persecuted, threatened with
jail terms, had careers shattered, lost family and housing and the like
for eating, say, Rocky Road ice cream, no one would ever eat it.
Everyone would pick another easily available flavor. That gay people
abided in being gay even in the face of such persecution in the recent
past suggests that being gay is not a matter of easy choice.

On the other hand, even if establishing a sexual orientation is not
like making a relatively trivial choice, perhaps it is relevantly like making the central and serious life choices by which individuals try to establish themselves as being of some type or having some occupation.
Again, if one examines gay experience, or at least gay male experience,
this seems not to be the case. For one virtually never sees anyone setting
out to become a homosexual, in the way one sees people setting out to
become doctors, lawyers, and bricklayers. One does not find gays-to-be
picking some end—"at some point in the future, I want to become a
homosexual"—and then setting about planning and acquiring the ways
and means to that end, in the way one sees people deciding that they
want to become lawyers, and then sees them planning what courses to
take and what sort of temperaments, habits, and skills to develop in
order to become lawyers. Typically gays-to-be simply find themselves

having homosexual encounters and yet, at least initially, resisting the identification of being homosexual. Such a person even very likely resists having such encounters, but ends up having them anyway. Only with time, luck, and personal effort, but sometimes never, does the person gradually come to accept her or his orientation, to view it as a given material condition of life, coming as materials do with certain capacities and limitations. The person begins to act in accordance with his or her orientation and its capacities, seeing its actualization as a requisite for an integrated personality and as a central component of personal well-being. As a result, the experience of coming out to oneself has for gays the basic structure of a discovery, not the structure of a choice. And far from signaling immorality, coming out to others affords one of the few remaining opportunities in ever more bureaucratic, technological, and socialistic societies to manifest courage.

To be fair, not a few lesbian feminists believe that being a lesbian is a choice, in particular a political choice.[22] This view, at least, has to hurdle the fact that sexual arousal is something which comes over a person. It is a passion, not an act of will like pulling a lever in a voting booth. So with this caveat, even this lesbian feminist stance differs from the fundamentalists' view that homosexuality is a (bad) habit, one caused by sexual pleasure which, in their view, rivets the initial sexual desire to the soul and so turns it into a conditioned response, an inclination, a propensity.

\* \* \*

How would society at large be changed if gays were socially accepted? Suggestions to change social policy with regard to gays are invariably met with claims that to do so would invite the destruction of civilization itself. After all isn't that what did Rome in? Actually, Rome's decay paralleled not the flourishing of homosexuality but its repression under the later Christianized emperors.

Still, the charge that gays are bent on destroying civilization is surprisingly persistent. In 1989, the U.S. Navy offered up a theory of a gay suicide bomber to explain the explosion of a gun-turret on the USS *Iowa* that killed forty-seven sailors. The navy alleged that one of the dead, Clayton Hartwig, was a suicidal closet-case, who blew up himself and his fellow sailors to cover up the shame he felt at being gay. The charge turned out to be baseless.[23] When in 1999 Vermont's supreme court ruled that the state had, in one way or another, to give same-sex couples rights and benefits identical to those given different-sex married couples, Republican presidential candidate and longtime "family values" advocate Gary L. Bauer said that the decision was "worse than terrorism."[24] Two days after the September 11, 2001, terrorist attacks on the Pentagon and World Trade Center, the Rev. Jerry Falwell declared on Pat Robertson's religious television program *The 700 Club* that gay rights proponents and abortion providers have "got to take a lot of the blame for this because God will not be mocked," that these groups had so weakened America's morality that God "lifted the curtain of protection" from around the country allowing the terrorists in: "I point the finger in their face and say, 'you helped this happen.'"[25] If the U.S. Navy, Gary Bauer, and Jerry Falwell laid such charges against any other group, Jews, for instance, everyone would recognize the charges as blood libels.

But even so, predictions of American civilization's imminent demise have been as premature as they have been frequent. Civilization has shown itself to be rather resilient here, in large part because of the country's traditional commitments to respect for privacy, to individual liberties, and especially to people minding their own business. These all give society an open texture and the flexibility to try out things to see what works. And because of this, we now need not speculate about what changes reforms in gay social policy might bring to society at large. For many reforms have already been tried.

By the time the Supreme Court declared sodomy laws unconstitutional in 2003, two-thirds of the states had through their own legislative or judicial branches decriminalized same-sex sex acts. Empirical studies have shown that there was no increase in other crimes in these states.

Neither has the passage of legislation barring discrimination against gays ushered in the end of civilization. More than one hundred counties and municipalities, including some of the country's largest cities (like Chicago, Los Angeles, and New York City) have passed such statutes barring discrimination in housing, employment, and public accommodations, as have, by 2003, fourteen states: Wisconsin, Massachusetts, Connecticut, Hawaii, New Jersey, Vermont, Minnesota, New Hampshire, Nevada, Rhode Island, Maryland, New York, New Mexico, and California. Four of these states—Minnesota, Rhode Island, New Mexico, and California—also protect "gender identity," which is to say a person's being or being perceived as transsexual, transgendered, transvestite, or ambiguously gendered. Again, no more brimstone has fallen in any of these places than elsewhere.

Berkeley, California, in 1984, followed by a couple dozen other cities including New York, passed "domestic partner" legislation giving same-sex couples at least some of the same rights to city benefits that heterosexually married couples have, and yet Berkeley has not become more weird than it already was. In 2000, Vermont, prompted by a decision of its supreme court the previous year, passed "civil union" legislation giving gay and lesbian couples all the same rights and obligations as heterosexually married couples. In 2003 and 2004, respectively, California and New Jersey gave same-sex couples access to the core rights and obligations of marriage through legislation establishing "domestic partnership" registries. Most northern European countries have instituted civil union arrangements for same-sex couples—Denmark in 1989 and later Finland, France, Germany, Greenland, Iceland, Norway, and Sweden. In 2000, the Netherlands, followed by Belgium, gave their citizens who were members of lesbian and gay couples access to marriage in full.[26] Also in 2000, Brazil gave members of same-sex couples the right to inherit each other's pension and social security benefits.[27] The highest courts in three Canadian provinces have legalized gay marriage there— Ontario (2003), British Columbia (2003), and Quebec (2004).[28] In April 2004, the newly elected, left-of-center prime minister of Spain—yes, the country that brought us the Inquisition—announced his country would follow Belgium and the Netherlands by providing same-sex couples access to civil marriage.[29] England and Wales are inching toward civil unions for same-sex couples.[30]

In November 2003, Massachusetts's highest court ruled that by May 17, 2004, the state had to start issuing marriage licenses to gay and lesbian couples. It then fortified its ruling in February 2004 by clarifying that a separate-but-equal civil union arrangement for gay and lesbian couples, like Vermont's, would not pass constitutional muster as a substitute for same-sex couples having access to marriage.[31] On May 17, 2004, 1,700 same-sex couples took out marriage licenses in the commonwealth.[32]

In the private sector, a number of major universities (including Harvard, Stanford, the University of Chicago, and Southern Methodist University) are offering their employees domestic partnership benefits, as are, in increasing numbers, large and even conservative corporations, like Walt Disney Studios, Mobil Oil, Merrill Lynch, Delta Airlines, Boeing, General Motors, Ford, Coors Brewing, even Wal-Mart.[33] Between 1992 and 2004, the number of Fortune 500 companies doing so shot up from twelve to more than two hundred.[34] Even more—78 percent—have nondiscriminatory policies for gay and lesbian employees.[35]

One virtually unnoticed area of private-sector progress has occurred in the most surprising of quarters—the insurance industry. Surprising, because insurance companies are inherently conservative institutions. Their well-being and very existence depend upon the usual, the normal, the average, the steady, the predictable. Only cats hate change more. Yet during the 1990s, most insurance carriers began offering domestic partner benefits under group coverage. It used to be that companies and towns with domestic partnership statutes were unable to find any insurer at all willing to carry their health policies. Now they have the luxury of competitive bids. The Allstate Insurance Company, a division of Sears, now writes homeowners policies for same-sex couples that are identical to those for heterosexually married couples. The Prudential Insurance Company, the nation's largest life insurance carrier, began offering its employees domestic-partnership benefits in 1999. The same year, the conservative Chubb Group of Insurance Companies blitzed the mailboxes of gay and lesbian yuppie couples across the nation with six-color brochures inviting them to insure their art and antiques with Chubb, a provider of "major funding" for PBS's *Antiques Roadshow*. On the last page, the brochure offers seven bulleted reasons why the Chubb Group is "gay friendly"—its phrase. This private-sector progress is leading rather than following general governmental trends.

Seemingly hysterical predictions that the American family would collapse if such reforms would pass have proven false, just as the same dire predictions that the availability of divorce would lessen the ideal and desirability of marriage proved unfounded. Indeed if current discrimination, which drives gays into hiding and into anonymous relations, ended, far from seeing gays destroying American families, one would see gays forming them. Studies have found that virtually all gay men and lesbians express a desire to have a permanent lover. Yet, society makes gay coupling difficult. It is hard for people to live together as couples without having their sexual orientation perceived in the public realm, which in turn targets them for discrimination. Sharing a life in hiding is even more constricting than life in a small nuclear family. Members of nongay couples are here asked to imagine what it would take to erase every trace of their own sexual orientation for even just one week.

Still, if nothing else, the groundswell of gay marriages made suddenly possible by San Francisco's and Portland, Oregon's, municipal and county disobedience in the spring of 2004 shows how committed to commitment gays are. Nearly 100 percent of the same-sex couples issued licenses in San Francisco between February 12 and March 11 when California's supreme court suspended the issuing of them— 3,955 out of 4,037 couples—subsequently returned to city hall to register their licenses with the city after solemnization, showing that the city hall celebrations were not publicity stunts, mere political acts, or cases of people being swept up in the moment.[36] During the seven weeks of March–April 2004 in which Multnomah County (Portland), Oregon, issued marriage licenses to same-sex couples, 6,000 people availed themselves of the opportunity.[37]

Society makes gay coupling difficult, but those lesbian and gay male couples who have survived the odds show that the structure of more usual couplings is not a matter of destiny, but of personal responsibility. The so-called basic unit of society turns out not to be a unique immutable atom, but can adopt different parts and be adapted to different needs.

If discrimination ceased, gay men and lesbians would enter the mainstream of the human community openly and with self-respect.

The energies that the typical gay person wastes in the anxiety of leading a day-to-day existence of systematic disguise would be released for use in personal flourishing. From this release would be generated the many spin-off benefits that accrue to a society when its individual members thrive.

Society would be richer for accepting another aspect of human diversity. Families with gay members would develop relations based on truth, trust, and openness rather than lies, embarrassment, or fear. And the heterosexual majority would be better off for knowing that they are no longer trampling their gay friends and neighbors.

Finally and perhaps paradoxically, in extending to gay men and lesbians the rights and benefits it has reserved for its dominant culture, America would confirm its deeply held vision of itself as a morally progressing nation, a nation itself advancing and serving as a beacon for others—especially with regard to human rights. The words with which our national pledge ends—"with liberty and justice for all"—are not a description of the present, but a call for the future. America is a nation prone to a prophetic political rhetoric which believes that morality is principled, not arbitrary, and that justice is more than the transient massings of a collective will. It is this vision that led the black civil rights movement to its successes. Those senators and representatives who opposed that movement and its centerpiece, the 1964 Civil Rights Act, on obscurantist grounds, but who lived long enough and were noble enough came in time to express their heartfelt regret and shame at what they had done. It is to be hoped and someday to be expected that those who now grasp at anything to oppose the extension of that which is best about America to lesbians and gay men will one day feel the same.

We can already see such a transformation at work within the Supreme Court. In a coda to his 2003 *Lawrence* decision overturning the Court's 1986 *Bowers* case, which had upheld sodomy laws, Justice Anthony Kennedy cast the new decision as a redemptive moment in the history of American law: "Had those who drew and ratified the [Constitution's] Due Process Clauses ... known the components of liberty in its manifold possibilities, they might have been more specific [than they were in articulating its range]. They did not presume to have this insight. They knew times can blind us to certain truths and later generations can see that laws once thought necessary and proper in fact serve only to oppress."

Who is the "we" in Kennedy's "us" here? Well, one suspects that in the first instance Kennedy is thinking of himself. When in 1987 he was elevated from the Ninth Circuit Court of Appeals to the Supreme Court, he brought with him a solidly antigay record. In all four gay cases in which he had a recorded vote as a circuit court judge, he voted against gays.[38] These cases covered military policy, privacy, employment, family issues, and immigration.[39]

In one case, he affirmed the firing of an openly gay federal civil servant on the grounds that to employ an openly gay person would hold the government up to shame. In *Lawrence*, Kennedy says just the opposite—"the State cannot demean [homosexuals'] existence." In the military case, Kennedy's opinion upheld the Defense Department's discharge of gay men and lesbians from the armed forces based not on anything lesbians and gay men do, but on the disruptions possibly caused by *other* people's dislike of gay men and lesbians. In fact, his opinion provided the wording for the department's exclusionary policy from 1981 to 1993. And perhaps most surprising to the reader of *Lawrence*, Kennedy's opinion in an immigration case upheld the deportation of a gay man, claiming that the deportation's destruction of the man's twelve-year marital-like relation with his life-partner would not count as an "extreme hardship," a condition that, by statute, would have barred the deportation. With no independent analysis, Kennedy simply adopted INS's conclusion that the relationship either counted for nothing in its own terms or should be analogized to a relationship of mere commercial dependence. In 2003, Kennedy held the opposite and gave constitutional recognition to the "enduring" and "personal bonds" of gay couples.

So it appears that in his own life, Kennedy has compressed into a mere eighteen years the span between blind times past and later generations possessed of insight into the more specific components of liberty. Gays and our supporters should hope that the rest of the nation crosses over this bridge as quickly.

\* \* \*

Justice Kennedy's *Lawrence v. Texas* opinion is an important moment in the discussion of lesbian and gay issues in America. It even provides a national symbol of change on these issues. And it is an important moment in the Supreme Court's thinking about itself in relation to lesbians and gay men. But as an analysis of the right to privacy and of the right's application to (homo)sexual cases, the decision is woefully deficient. I address this deficiency in the next chapter.

## Chapter 2

## Sexual Privacy

America doesn't like to talk about sex. I suspect that one impulse driving America's rush to conceptualize lesbians and gay men as a religious- or ethnic-like minority is to avoid having to do that very thing. And what with all the talk of gay marriage in the air, a space alien anthropologist recently come to Earth would hardly suspect that sex was part of what defined gay men and lesbians as homosexuals. Keep an eye out for "Love Waits" pledge cards to start showing up at gay community centers. The age of the Great Gay Secondary Virginity is upon us. I exaggerate—but only slightly. If a five-second exposure of a beautiful, exquisitely coifed right breast during a Super Bowl half-time entertainment can cause a vertigo of congressional panic and media mea culpas in 2004 America, then we can safely say that anyone who thought that after the 1969 Stonewall Riots the "gay liberation movement" was going to liberate sexuality and lead it to be socially viewed as a freestanding good, well, that person has long since been sorely disappointed.

In keeping with the times, Justice Kennedy, in his June 2003 *Lawrence v. Texas* decision, talks as little about sex as he can possibly get away with. In overturning the Supreme Court's 1986 *Bowers v. Hardwick* case and its upholding of sodomy laws from privacy challenges, Kennedy is much more comfortable talking about gay social history than about gay sex, or indeed any sex.[1] The argumentative core of the case is terse and cryptic, but clear enough to see that Kennedy tries to justify gay sex only by romanticizing it and cabining it within marital-like relations.

The core privacy analysis telescopes into just two, inelegant sentences: "To say that the issue in *Bowers* was simply the right to engage in certain sexual conduct demeans the claim the [homosexual] individual put forward, just as it would demean a married couple were it to be said marriage is simply about the right to have sexual intercourse. . . . When sexuality finds overt expression in intimate conduct with another person, the conduct can be but one element in a personal bond that is more enduring."[2] Gay men and lesbians get to have sex because of the role sex plays in their bonds "more enduring," their long-term emotional relationships.

Kennedy, a Roman Catholic, is here trying to adapt and apply to gay relationships the Catholic doctrine that a marriage unconsummated is not a marriage at all.[3] Sex is here redeemed only by its role within a marital-like relation. But it is not clear, then, why all possible types of sexual acts should be protected as being necessary for this consummative role. After all, the doctrine itself justifies only one type of sex act in different-sex marriages, one in which same-sex couples do not engage—at that. Further, the Texas "deviate sexual intercourse" statute which the Supreme Court voided in *Lawrence* had been written so precisely and narrowly in an effort to elude being held "void for vagueness" that it left perfectly legal a slew of acts which people consider sexual and which gays could use for consummative purposes understood more broadly than procreational ones. Ironically: the kinkier the sex act the less likely it was to be covered by the "deviate sexual intercourse" statute.

Embarrassingly, Kennedy's romanticizing analysis, which argues that sexual acts are protected just *to the extent that* they are a necessary part of a marital-like personal relationship, does not actually cover the sodomitic act between John Geddes Lawrence and Tyron Garner that launched the constitutional challenge to the Texas law in the first place. Discretion and circumspection alone were not what prompted Kennedy to pass over in silence the facts of the case. The lawyers for Lawrence and Garner were lucky to have kept the men under wraps as the case worked its way through the courts. Like the sexual encounter for which Michael Hardwick's arrest was upheld in *Bowers v. Hardwick*, the sexual spark to *Lawrence* was casual, not a part of an enduring personal bond. Lawrence and Garner never were a couple. The person with whom Garner *had* had an enduring personal bond was the man who on a vindictive, false accusation of weapons' violations sent the police into Lawrence's apartment where Lawrence and Garner were having anal sex and who had earlier been granted a temporary restraining order against Garner based on charges of sexual battery in *their* enduring personal relationship. Not a pretty picture.[4]

While the *Lawrence* decision may have important social and cultural consequences as a banner or advertisement for change, conceptually, normatively, and legally speaking there is, as Tallulah Bankhead would put it, "less here than meets the eye." We need to start almost from scratch in considering the proper relations between sexual acts and sexual privacy.

\* \* \*

It is noteworthy that over a very broad spectrum of political opinion, people agree that there is a general right to privacy. In the broad middle band of the political spectrum, including liberals and conservatives alike and all the currently live political positions in the United States, everyone agrees that there is a right to privacy. But disagreement breaks out over what specific protections this general right encompasses. Liberals view it as entailing such protections as a right to abortion, a right to own pornography, and possibly even a right to own drugs; conservatives view it rather as encompassing such rights as a right to unrestricted use of property, a right to own automatic weapons, and a right to conduct business with whomever one wants. In this chapter, I assume, along with the rest of the nation, that there is a right to privacy.

I then give three diverse moral arguments that each independently explain why consensual sex acts engage a dimension of privacy in a way that invokes privacy as a right.

\* \* \*

The breadth of agreement over the existence of a right to privacy is (I believe) a tacit acknowledgment that privacy rights in part derive from the very nature of human agency, more particularly from the fact that, unlike angels, we have bodies, indeed in some sense *are* our bodies. The distinctive relation that a person holds to his or her body grounds an important dimension of sexual privacy and of privacy more generally. What one does to one's body or has done to one's own body has a special status underwritten by the importance of the body itself.

The body is the foundation for a person's being in the world at all, for his projection of himself into the world through actions, and for his instilling value in things. The body is not merely necessary for existence and action—as food, shelter, and a kidney machine might be—but also is part of that *in virtue of which* a person is and acts. If a person is to be free in any of her actions, she must therefore have control of her own body—not in the sense of doing *with* it as she will, but doing *to* it as she will—so that it is hers. In order that an action is one's own, it is not enough that the action be the product of one's intentions. For one's intentions are presented not merely by and through but inextricably *with* one's body. Therefore, if a person's acts are to be his own, his body as well as his intentions must be his own.

Now, no one could assert that a person's thoughts and intentions were really her own—formed the basis of a free action—if they were the thoughts she just happened to have, if, for instance, they were simply installed there in her mind by brainwashing, electrodes, or God. And they would not even be her own if she fell into them by chance—if they just happened to be "in the air" and she passively absorbed them. The ideas would be her own in a significant sense only if she had considered them, worked them over, appropriated them, and especially if she produced them new. Without the last, at least as a possibility, a person's thoughts are not truly his own.

Similarly, if a person's existence is to be her own other than by accident and if her actions are to be free, her body must not belong to her merely by accident. A person must not be forced merely to accept what is given by nature or by others' volitions. He must be permitted the opportunity to mold it, shape it, alter it, and even to make it as boldly new as it is capable, not as others allow, assuming, of course, all the usual restraints on what he may do *to* others *with* it. A person cannot reshape his fist by breaking it on another's skull. A person may not be able to cut her hand at all if that would cause her preemptively to fail of some duty justifiably incumbent upon her—say, military service in defensive war. But such relatively clear exceptions aside, a person must be free to do to his body as he sees fit, if he is to be free at all.

Another route to the same conclusion is to notice that a person's body is not just one more damn thing in the world that she might have or own, but rather has a special value and standing, as that *in virtue of which* she possesses other things and as the chief means by which other things come to have value. "My body" has a wholly different status than even "my house." A house belongs to its owner because he built it with his body or bought it with fruits of the labor his body provided him. An unappropriated object in the world becomes one's own as one mixes one's labor with it, for it would then be unjust for anyone else to take it. No one else in this circumstance deserves it.[5]

A person's property rights then devolve from a special status that she has as a body. If some of the world is her own, it is so because of her body. The body is not merely a necessary condition for a person's appropriating what is her own, it is also the chief causal condition for appropriation. If one speaks of one's body as "mine," it is nevertheless not subject to the same restraints and controls as other things that one owns, for it is morally and causally prior to their being one's own.

A person's body is therefore not available to government for its legitimate projects in the way her (other) property is. Government cannot prevent the individual from valuing herself and possessing herself and yet still suppose that—at least in some areas such as those protected by substantive rights—she is not merely a tool of and for government, but has her own projects and values that take precedence. If there are any substantive liberties, a person has a right to instill value in herself and possess herself.

A very powerful right to privacy then is generated by and over the body because of its special status in one's projects, one's values, and one's very presence in the world. As the means by which one both projects oneself into the world and appropriates what is one's own to oneself, the body engenders special protections for one's actions that chiefly affect it, even if the features of the world which it affects, produces, or appropriates are not covered by the same right and thus remain generally subject to state control.

The general right to control one's body has at its core a cluster of specific bodily based liberties: one has a strong presumptive right to feed one's body, to manipulate it, to exercise it, to dress it as one sees fit, to seek medical treatment, to inject foreign bodies into it, to permit others to do so, to touch it, to have others touch it, to allow others to present their bodies to it, and to be the chief governor and guarantor of one's own feelings, emotions, and sensations—compatible with a like ability on the part of others and with other requirements for civil society. Consensual sex engages and nearly exhausts the core protections of the general right to bodily based privacy. Indeed it comes close to being a perfect or complete exemplification of its provisions.

Only when one's control of one's body is protected, does one have a right to bodily integrity, and only when one has bodily integrity is one a person at all. Any moral systems, then, in which persons are a locus of value will be obliged to protect from government those persons' acts of consensual sex.

Privacy rights understood in this way would actually have protected the sex that Lawrence and Geddes were having as well as other sodomitic sex acts conducted outside the marital bed. It is true that a marriage unconsummated is not a marriage at all—I explain why below—but more sex acts than those conducted within marriage or marriage-like relations are covered by the right to privacy.

Justice Harry Blackmun's four-member dissent in *Bowers v. Hardwick* turned on rights to the control of one's body and one's sensations. A right to "bodily integrity," a "right to physical autonomy," and "the urgent claim of a person to retain the ultimate control over her body" jointly formed one of two independent bases for the right to abortion articulated in the Court's most recent examination of the constitutional underpinning of this right—*Planned Parenthood v. Casey* (1992).[6] Justice Kennedy had these powerful resources available to him, but he disregarded them, and so came up with an inadequate and intellectually puny decision.

* * *

The specific sort of "doings to oneself" that count as sexual in addition suggest that there is a privacy inherent in sex acts. In their form, sex acts are "world excluding": custom and taboo aside, sexual arousal and activity, like the activities of reading a poem or praying alone, propel away the ordinary world, the everyday workaday world of public places, public function, and public observation. They do so in several ways.

First, sexually aroused people experience the world in an altered way. Sexual arousal alters perception of reality in some of the same ways powerful drugs do. Space recedes. Arousal is an immersion into a different medium, as into sleep fraught with scary possibilities, or as into a liquid.

In continued arousal, perception becomes more and more focused and narrow. One attends only to what is near. One's gaze no longer roams or scans at large. The focusing process calls for and is enhanced by nightfall. Only what is near, if any thing at all, is seen. Gradually, perception is channeled away from vision—the supreme sense of the everyday public world—a sense that requires a gulf of open space between perceiver and perceived. Perception shifts from vision to touch—the sense that requires the absence of open space. At peak arousal, as in a blizzard, the horizon is but the extent of one's flesh. One is hermetic save for the continuation of one's flesh with the flesh of another.

No less, sex withdraws one from the world of waking and talking, from reason, persuasion, and thought. Sex is essentially a world of silence; words, such as they are, are not reports, descriptions, or arguments, but murmurs and invocations that emphasize silence and its awe.

Time, like space, recedes with arousal. Suspended is the time by which one gauges the regularity and phases of the workaday world.

Time is interrupted and becomes inconsequential, as in the spontaneity and attention-absorbing fascination of games.

Second, social relations alter importantly during the shift into erotic reality; people with whom one has functional, public roles fade away entirely or at least as persons strictly identified with those roles. Colleagues and service personnel fade from consciousness. One becomes focused only upon those who potentially jibe with one's tastes, the particularities of one's erotic choices and desires.

Third, in the process of sexual arousal, one becomes increasingly incarnate, submerged in the flesh. When this process is mutual and paired with the shift in perception to touch, it achieves an unparalleled intimacy. In sexual disengagement from spatial, social, and psychological circumstances, the body ceases to be merely a coat hanger for personality. It assumes an independent life of its own.

One perceives the other as flesh and desires the other to be flesh. Usually one becomes, in turn, flesh for another, in part because one's own submersion into the flesh sparks or enhances desire in the other. The recognition of this effect on the other, in turn again, facilitates one's own further submersion. As this process repeats, one eventually becomes just the body sensing. This sexually aroused body, in turn, distills and transforms the sensations typical of the everyday world. A touch, say, a light brushing of the flesh, that would go largely unnoticed in the everyday world, save possibly for its social significance, here becomes an intense yet diffuse pleasure.

Fourth, the everyday world of will and deeds fades away with sexual arousal. The will is not a chief causal factor in the fulfillment of sexual desire. Indeed, quite the opposite is true: the willing of sexual arousal guarantees it will not occur. Sexual arousal must happen *to* one; it is a passion, not an action, project, or deed. It can only occur in situations in which one is not observing one's progress and judging how one is doing. Self-observation, self-judging, and the willing of arousal are the chief causes of—and virtually guarantee—impotence. One has to be lost in the sex for it to work upon one.

The slide into the purely sensing body and the immediacy and simultaneity of touching and being touched produce a transparency in the flow of information and sensation between partners. The vagueness and ambiguity typical of everyday interactions are here refined into a clarity of cause and effect unmatched in human experience. One is as intimate as one could be.

For all these reasons, the sexual realm is inherently private. The sex act creates its own sanctuary, which in turn is necessary for its success. The whole process and nature of sex is interrupted and destroyed if penetrated by the glance of an intruder, an uninvited observer. Like the telephone ringing, such observation brings crashing in its train the everyday world of duration and distance, function and duty, will and action. Most importantly, such observation judges—even if sympathetically—causing self-reflection. Such reflection may only generate a sense of uncertainty, but it virtually always causes a great deal more disruption. For, where a socially imposed obligation to maintain an act as secret mounts to the level of taboo (as is the case with sexual behavior in America), *any* observation, even a seemingly disinterested one, is bound to be construed by the observed as a harsh intrusive judgment. There is no such thing as casual observation of people at rut.

To observe sex, but not participate in it, is to violate the sexual act. Sex's form makes it inherently private. Any moral theory that protects privacy as sanctuary and as repose from the world must presumptively protect sexual activity.

* * *

Beyond sex's formal attributes, the function, end, and fulfillment of erotic behavior also provide grounds for thinking that sex is private—private in the sense of "the personal," where the personal means a nonarbitrary, nonidiosyncratic set of central, personally affecting interests. The manner of realizing such central interests is left up to the person who has them, since the personal in this sense is viewed culturally as one's own affair by right. The interests that are the aim, goal, and function of one's erotic choices and behavior—including the choice not to engage in sexual behavior—meet this level of centrality.

Sexual impulses are directed toward the fulfillment not only of desires but also of needs. Though the fulfillment of sexual drives is not necessary to the continued biological existence of an individual, as are some things that are called natural needs, sexual desire (unlike addictions) recurs independent of its satisfaction. It is a desire that, if one has it at all, constantly presses itself upon life no matter what one does. Taken at face value traditional sodomy laws would block entirely any sex life for gay men and lesbians; in practice they tended more to contribute to social forces that instill guilt into sexual behavior rather than to stop sexual behavior. Either way though—through repression or guilt—bans on sexual life curdle and poison the soul. They contribute to people becoming harsh, hard, brittle, obsessive, and alienated. The intrusiveness and perpetual return of sexual desire means that for a healthy personality, the total forgoing of a sex life would itself have to be a major life commitment, possible only if the resignation were itself voluntary—as in the case of nuns and priests, for whom vows of chastity are as central as any vows they take. Mere external restraint could never produce "virtue" here.

Yet, it is not merely as a need that sexual pleasure is central to human life. In both intensity and kind, it is unique among human pleasures. It has no passable substitute from other realms of life. For ordinary persons—not mystics or adolescent poets—orgasmic sex is the only access they have to ecstasy. This may take a number of forms: self-transcendence, a "standing outside of self " (which is ecstasy's etymological sense); melting and fusion; engulfing embrace; quiet peace; and self-negation, or what the French euphemistically call an orgasm—"the little death." All of these modes of ecstasy have clear counterparts only in religious visions of the end of life and the ends of life. If pleasure is its own bottom, then sex as the most intense of pleasures is one of the central freestanding components of the good life. Not only must sex be central as a need, it ought to stand centrally as what for most persons causes them to feel the most alive.

Further, if marital love is central to the good life, sex will be central for this reason as well—quite independent of its role in procreation. The relation of sex to love is like the relation of a figured bass to a piece of music with a figured bass or, more so, the repeating bass line of a passacaglia to the passacaglia as a whole, providing the piece both its harmonic and melodic materials, its depth and the pulse. Sex is a necessary part and positive contribution to marital relations; it supports and shapes the whole as a foundation does a house. And this is why friendships for whatever their emotional and spiritual intensity lack the warmth and depth of love relationships. Even if only as possible or recollected, sex acts are the pedal points and diapason of love relationships. This recognition is the kernel of truth left in the religious belief that a marriage unconsummated is not a marriage at all. In blocking gays from having sex, the state would also deny them love. The importance of sex to the good life should make it clear that privacy in sexual matters is central to a person's right to the pursuit of happiness.

\* \* \*

How do these results redound on the government's ability to address the ongoing problem of AIDS? The earliest years of the twenty-first century saw an increase in the percentage of new HIV exposures that resulted from gay men having unprotected sex. After a decade of declining AIDS rates among gay men, gay men were again coming down with AIDS disproportionately to their numbers in the general population, even though they are fully aware of how HIV is transmitted.[7] The Internet was credited with facilitating such unsafe sex, and there even developed among some gay men a cult psychology that romanticized, even mythologized, condomless anal sex. The cult had its own cant. Unsafe anal sex was called "barebacking" or "skin on skin" sex. Some gay men with HIV actively sought out uninfected men in order to infect—or in the cant, "seed"—them, and some uninfected gay men actively sought out the infected with the purpose of becoming infected. The virus itself was referred to by these two groups as "the gift." Many more gay men, weary of being consciously on guard all the time in an area where the mind's very inclination is to "let go," simply dropped their guard. Government-funded safe-sex literature never moved much beyond schoolmarmish moralizing, even when it was trying to be cute: "Never go out without your rubbers." The gay community's own attempts to develop an eroticized vision of condom use ran into strong headwinds from both nature and culture.

What did develop within the gay male community were deep streaks of self-hatred caused or magnified by forces around AIDS. Even wise people, like Larry Kramer, could be found wallowing in self-recrimination as they hurled against gay men the very rhetoric of "Nature hates you" that the Christian Right hurls there: "We brought AIDS upon ourselves by a way of living that welcomed it. Nature always extracts a price for sexual promiscuity. Tragically not enough of us have responded to this information maturely and responsibly."[8] Not surprisingly then, some gay men and others are calling on the state to use its power paternalistically to force "mature" living upon gay men, whom they consider infantile, to force them to do what they won't do on their own— for their own good. Consider nationally syndicated gay columnist Dan Savage's perky call for government officials to close gay bathhouses: "The only appropriate health message around bathhouses is 'Don't go,' and the health departments know it and they won't say it because they are afraid of being called homophobic. Well, boo-fucking-hoo, they are the health department. Somebody has got to be daddy and somebody has got to stop worrying about what they will be seen as."[9]

To America's credit, the country only flirted with two coercive measures widely proposed early in the era of AIDS—quarantines (which have pretty much occurred only in prison settings) and compulsory HIV testing (which two states briefly made a condition for securing marriage licenses).

But there are two other areas in which coercive measures have spread widely and are likely to spread farther—the closing of bathhouses in which gay men have impersonal sexual encounters and the criminalizing of an HIV-positive person's knowingly having unprotected sex with an uninfected person. Both these uses of state coercion are impermissible if sexual behavior is covered by a right. Privacy rights take sexuality out of the box of tools that society can use to advance its projects and place it into the sphere where a person is accountable just to himself for his well-being. To have a right means to be sovereign over the area covered by the right. A right removes that area from the government's calculations of social utility.

On March 25, 2004, the *Los Angeles Times* editorialized for the closing of that city's eleven bathhouses. It claimed that one does not have a right to go to a bathhouse, even if one has a right to have sex. But state closures of bathhouses are not being promoted as a means of advancing a social good other than inhibiting an activity that is protected by right. The proposed closures are not like a content-neutral "time, place, or manner regulation" of, say, a rock concert, aimed at some end other than eliminating the musicians' ability to express themselves. A rule that says "no open-air concerts above 150 decibels after 10 P.M." has the aim of letting the neighbors sleep, rather than suppressing the rise of rock stars. But in the bathhouse case, the closures seek to achieve their end—reducing the spread of HIV infection—just exactly by targeting the very activity that is covered by right. To say one has a right to have sex, but not to have it in a bathhouse, is like saying that one has a right to drink alcohol, but not a right to buy it. You could after all make your own. The only reason for barring the sale of alcohol is to disrupt the drinking of it. So too the only legitimate end achieved by closing the bathhouses is achieved by stopping something that people do by right. Notice that no one has seriously suggested shutting down the Internet because gay men use it to "hook up" for unsafe sex.

It might be claimed that by contributing to an increase in the general rate of HIV infection in the population, bathhouses burden the public purse and so cause indirect harms to others that mount to the level of being a violation of the others' rights, and so justify bathhouse closings. Such moves try to skirt around making appeals to paternalism—the coercing of a person for his of her own good. America has seen such skirting in other contexts. Some liberal politicians have, through similar appeals to remote harms, backed laws mandating seat belt use: people who don't wear seatbelts, though they directly harm only themselves when they fly through windshields at seventy miles an hour, indirectly harm others by ending up in public hospitals and nursing homes or otherwise on the public dole, causing everyone's taxes to increase. But a person does not have a right to low taxes, no more so than a person has a right to low milk prices. If I go to the store and find that the price of milk has gone up two cents, I am worse off for that—my dollar will now not stretch as far as before—and I may be unhappy, even miffed, at the change, but my rights have not been violated. And so I cannot legitimately insist on a ban on whatever led to the raised milk price. Not every bad thing that happens to me violates my rights. So too, society may well be less well off if people have unprotected sex; the populace at large is likely to pay higher taxes, but this does not violate anyone's rights, and so does not in turn justify coercively regulating an activity that otherwise occurs by right.

Taking seriously the position that people have the right to put themselves at risk for fatal illnesses does not make for great publicity when trying to promote increased funding for medical research into these very illnesses. But then no one said that we should cease funding research on cardiac diseases just because fat cat businessmen eat too much and exercise too little.

The other area where the state has been actively using its police power to try to address AIDS is the passage of laws making it a felony for an HIV-positive person knowingly to have unprotected sex with another a person. A majority of states have adopted such laws, though they are enforced only sporadically and, then, almost always against segments of the population already dispossessed—prostitutes, drug addicts, the homeless. People try to justify these laws by arguing that someone who potentially exposes another to the virus is like a drunk driver or a person shooting randomly in a theater. But the element of self-exposure in HIV infection—you get it by doing something with someone who already has it—makes the disease's mode of transmission relevantly dissimilar to both of these other potentially fatal behaviors. Acts of will on the part of a bystander hit by a drunkenly driven car or the theatergoer struck by a bullet are not directed toward and do not actively participate in nor contribute to the course of events that harms these people. Their presence by the road or in the theater is merely a necessary condition for the harm—as are millions of other states of affairs, such as their being born in the first place. One would not say that it was in virtue of or on account of their actions that they were harmed. But one *would* say this of the person who gets AIDS through unprotected sexual contacts or shared needles knowing that the virus can be transmitted this way. He actively participated in the very course of action that harms him. His deeds are not merely necessary conditions for harm but contribute to the causal chain by which he is harmed. It was in virtue of his actions that harm came to him.

What about the case where someone lies about his HIV status and then goes ahead and has unprotected sex with the person who asked after that status? Though lying is a paradigmatically immoral act, typically it is not actionable at law. Here, what is crucial to notice is that lying in what is culturally construed as a personal interaction is not something that is punished by law. Lying in a commercial context is actionable. It is fraud. Lying in a judicial context is actionable. It is perjury. But if I lie to you when I tell you I'm going to come over tonight to pick you up for a date, your recourse, when I fail to show up, is not to call 911. So too for the person who lets a fellow insert his unclad penis into him because he asked the fellow who was about to do so whether he has HIV and he said "no"; this person does not have legitimate recourse to the law. Life has ugly, messy bits that are not the business of the police to unscramble. Many people will find this result unsettling, even repulsive, in this case, but it is where consistency leads.

If one takes seriously the idea that sexual behavior is protected by a fundamental right, then virtually all coercive measures that have been proposed and are currently being proposed to address AIDS through the use of the state's police powers are inappropriate. Rights are trumps over social utility. Rights throw grit into the smooth workings of society.[10] Rights give you the permission to pave your very own way to hell and limit the ways in which the state may save you from your own gullibility.[11] Therefore, society will have to address AIDS through nonpunitive, noncoercive means—like education, medical research, and the public provision of health care—even if many of these measures are at best not very effective when it comes to AIDS and even if these efforts are positively hampered by the political fallout from people leading their lives by their own lights as a matter of right.

\* \* \*

Traditionally, sex was thought properly to occur only within marriage. This chapter suggests that while sex is a prerequisite for a relationship to count as marital, sex need not occur within marriage to be worthy of the protection of rights. Though the Supreme Court's *Lawrence v. Texas* decision is inadequate as a general defense of the right to sexual privacy, the defense that it does give—its romanticizing of sexual acts—almost inevitably will lead, in the long run, to a recognition that the right to privacy also encompasses gay marriage. The *Lawrence* decision was careful to say that it was leaving the issue of gay marriage for another day, but consider again how its logic worked: homosexual sexual acts are protected by privacy rights because the acts have an instrumental role within enduring personal relationships *and* because these enduring personal relationships themselves are relevantly similar to (heterosexual) marital relations, which stand at the very center of privacy's protections. But then, to an even greater degree surely, the enduring personal relationships themselves must be protected by the right to privacy that protects (heterosexual) marriage to begin with, since it is only through the relationships that this privacy is transferred to the same-sex sex acts. Think of it this way. We are told, *as a conclusion*, that homo-sodomitic acts fall within the Van Allen Belts of privacy that encircle earthly (heterosexual) marriage and protect it from the solar flares of state power. And we are told, *as a premise*, that the acts fall inside these Van Allen Belts of privacy *just exactly because* they are part of enduring relationships. But the conclusion only follows from this premise if there is another tacit or suppressed premise: the enduring relationships themselves fall within the protective belts as well. To make this premise explicit is to have gay marriage protected by privacy through the reasoning of *Lawrence*.

Just five months after *Lawrence*, Massachusetts's highest court declared the state's different-sex-only marriage law unconstitutional.[12] The court did not do so in precisely the terms mapped out here. Indeed, the decision did next to nothing in precise terms. Still it should come as no surprise that the Massachusetts decision quoted *Lawrence*'s general language as soon as it possibly could, in its second paragraph. The court seemed to intuit what was implicit in *Lawrence*.

Whether the enduring personal relationships of lesbian and gay couples *are* relevantly like those of (heterosexually) married couples cannot be answered until we know what marriage is. Neither *Lawrence* nor any of the marriage cases on which it relies even attempt to answer this question. The main goal of the next chapter is to offer an analysis of marriage that adequately explains its nature. In turn, the chapter argues that its nature suits those gay and lesbian couples who want to get married just fine.

*Chapter 3*

## The Case for Lesbian and Gay Marriage

The climax of Harvey Fierstein's 1979 play *Torch Song Trilogy* is a dialogue—well, shouting match—between mother and son about traditional marriage and its gay variant. As is frequently the case, the nature and function of an institution flashes forth only when the institution breaks down or is dissolved—here by the death of Arnold's lover.

> [ARNOLD]: (I'm) widow-ing.
> … … …
>
> [MA]: Wait, wait, wait, wait, wait. Are you trying to compare my marriage with you and Alan? Your father and I were married for thirty-five years, had two children and a wonderful life together. You have the nerve to compare yourself to that?
> … … …
>
> What loss did you have? … Where do you come to compare that to a marriage of thirty-five years?
> … … …

It took me two months until I could sleep in our bed alone, a year to learn to say "I" instead of "we." Are you going to tell me you were "widowing." How dare you!

[ARNOLD]: You're right, Ma. How dare I. I couldn't possibly know how it feels to pack someone's clothes in plastic bags and watch the garbage-pickers carry them away. Or what it feels like to forget and set his place at the table. How about the food that rots in the refrigerator because you forgot how to shop for one? How dare I? Right, Ma? How dare I?

[MA]: May God strike me dead! Whatever I did to my mother to deserve a child speaking to me this way. The disrespect! ... .

[ARNOLD]: Listen, Ma, you had it easy. You have thirty-five years to remember, I have five. You had your children and friends to comfort you, I had me! My friends didn't want to hear about it. They said "What're you gripin' about? At least you had a lover." 'Cause everybody knows that queers don't feel nothin'. How dare I say I loved him? You had it easy, Ma. You lost your husband in a nice clean hospital, I lost mine out there. They killed him there on the street. Twenty-three years old, laying dead on the street. Killed by a bunch of kids with baseball bats. Children. Children taught by people like you. 'Cause everybody knows that queers don't matter! Queers don't love! And those that do deserve what they get! ...

* * *

Reality concurs with Fierstein's fictional account. Years of domesticity have made Brian and Ed familiar figures in the archipelago of middle-aged, middle-class couples who make up my village's permanent gay male community. Ed drives a city bus. Brian is a lineman for the power company—or rather he was until a freak accident set aflame the cherry-picker atop which he worked. He tried to escape by leaping to a nearby tree but lost his grip and landed on his head. Eventually, it becomes clear that Brian will be permanently brain-damaged. After a few awkward weeks in the hospital, Brian's parents don't let Ed visit anymore. Eventually they move Brian to their village and home, where Ed is not allowed.

If the government had through marriage allowed Brian and Ed to be next-of-kin to each other, the story would have had a different ending— one in keeping with our cultural belief that those to whom we as adults entrust our tendance in crisis are people we choose, our spouses, who love us because of who we are, not people who are thrust upon us by the luck of the draw and who may love us only in spite of who we are.

Gay and lesbian couples are living together as traditionally married people do, even though almost everywhere in America they are legally barred from getting married. The injustices this bar cause in these lives make the bar one that deserves a close examination.

*  *  *

We cannot know whether gay men and lesbians belong in the marrying kind until we know what marriage is. If one asks ordinary people what marriage is, they generally just get tongue-tied. The meaning of marriage is somehow supposed to be so obvious in our culture, so entrenched and ramified in daily life that it is never in need of articulation. Standard dictionaries, which track and make coherent common usages of terms, are unhelpfully circular. Most commonly, dictionaries define marriage in terms of spouses, spouses in terms of husband and wife, and husband and wife in terms of marriage. In consequence, the various definitions do no positive work in explaining what marriage is and so simply end up rawly assuming or stipulating that marriage must be between people of different sexes.

The legal definition of marriage fares no better. It derives from a 1974 Washington State case in which a gay couple wanting to get married pointed out that the state's marriage law did not actually specify the genders of the spouses mentioned in the law. Washington's supreme court stepped into the definitional breech and defined marriage as "the legal union of one man and one woman as husband and wife." This definition has become *the* legal definition of marriage. It was taken up into the standard legal lexicon, *Black's Law Dictionary*, and from there into federal law through 1996's so-called Defense of Marriage Act. And it is the definition that President Bush would have the nation write into the Constitution as a permanent and universal ban on gay marriage in America.

Yet, this definition has no content and explains nothing. First, the qualification "as husband and wife" is circular. Since (again) "husband" and "wife" *mean* people who are in a marriage with each other, the definition, as far as these terms go, presupposes the very thing to be defined—marriage. If we drop the circular part of the definition, we are left with marriage as *the* legal union of one man and one woman. "Legal" here does not just mean "not illegal" (as a post-prom smooch might be said to be the legal union of one man and one woman), rather "legal" here is short for "legally acknowledged" or "acknowledged in laws." Marriage, so understood, would then be the one and only relation between men and women that the law sets into a frame of laws, rights, and duties. But this definition fails to track legal reality: the law acknowledges other relations between men and women. Laws set up rights and obligations between men and women who are not married to each other but who have children with each other. And the law acknowledges gender-specific relations in some "Romeo and Juliet" laws: in a 1981 case, the U.S. Supreme Court upheld California's "Romeo and Juliet" law that sent to prison teenage boys who had sex with underage girls but not teenage girls who had sex with underage boys.[1]

But even if marriage were, by historical accident, the one and only legally acknowledged union between the sexes, we still would not know what the content of the union was that motivated the requirement that its members be of different sexes. Indeed we are told nothing of any sort about the content of "the union" that is supposed to be the heart of marriage. The definition is not only circular but vacuous as well. The formulation of the definition serves no other function than to exclude from marriage—whatever it is—the people whom America views as destroyers of the American family, same-sex couples and polygamists: "*one* man and *one* woman." Like the ordinary dictionary definitions, the legal definition does no explanatory work. It is a raw stipulation.

Perhaps sensing the shakiness of a stipulative definition of little or no content, the courts have tried to supplement the supposedly obvious requirement of gender disparity in access to marriage with appeal to reproduction. By assuming that "the procreation and rearing of children" is essential to married life, the courts have implicitly given marriage a functional definition designed to eliminate lesbians and gay men from the ranks of the marriageable. "As we all know" (the courts self-congratulatorily declare), lesbians are "constitutionally incapable" of bearing children by other lesbians, and gay men are incapable of siring children by other gay men.

But the legally acknowledged institution of marriage in fact does not match this functional definition. In his dissent to *Lawrence v. Texas*, Justice Antonin Scalia warned conservatives not to place too much hope on children serving as the saviors of marriage for heterosexuality: "What justification could there possibly be for denying the benefits of marriage to homosexual couples exercising 'the liberty protected by the Constitution'? Surely not the encouragement of procreation, since the sterile and the elderly are allowed to marry."[2]

The functional definition is too broad as well. If the function of marriage is to bear and raise children in a family context, then the state should have no objection to the legal recognition of polygamous marriages. Male-hubbed polygamous families have been efficient bearers of children; and the economies of scale afforded by polygamous families also make them efficient in the rearing of children. It is telling that the standard charge now laid against male polygamists is the same charge that has standardly been laid against male homosexuals—that they are child molesters.

So given the actual scope of legal marriage, reproduction and child rearing cannot be its purpose or primary justification. The assumption that child rearing is a function uniquely tethered to the institution of heterosexual marriage also collides with an important, but underacknowledged, social reality. Many lesbian and gay male couples already are raising families in which children are the blessings of adoption, artificial insemination, surrogacy, or prior marriages. Many more lesbians and gay men would like to raise or foster children—perhaps ones from among those alarming numbers of gay kids who have been beaten up and thrown out of their "families" for being gay. The country is experiencing something approaching a gay and lesbian baby boom. The 2000 federal census reported that 594,000 U.S. households were headed by same-sex couples, a figure considered by some experts to be low due to underreporting by couples who might not want the nature of their relationship known to the federal government. Of the recorded couples, about 33 percent of lesbian couples reported having children under nineteen years of age living with them, while 22 percent of male couples did.[3] One might well ask what conceivable purpose can be served for these children by barring to their gay and lesbian parents the mutual cohesion, emotional security, and economic benefits that are ideally promoted by legal marriage.

Courts in twenty states have created, if not quite gay marriages, at least legally acknowledged gay families, by allowing what are called second-parent adoptions.[4] In the typical case, one lesbian partner bears a child and then the other is allowed to adopt the child *without* the biological mother losing any parental rights. Such an adoption requires judges to set aside the long-established legal rule that when one person adopts a child, someone else has to lose parental rights over the child. Here, appeals to family law's "best interest of the child" test, which conservative judges (as we will see) have used as a club to beat up gay parents in custody and visitation battles, is used as part of a quiet revolution in family law.

This social and legal revolution in gay family law will likely soon be joined by a biological one that will enable gay (male) couples to sire and bear children that are in biology entirely and jointly the couple's own. In May 2003, scientists at the University of Pennsylvania reported in *Science* that they had turned stem cells from male mice into eggs.[5] It has long been known that placentas are entirely the product of the embryos they feed, not their hosts; all they need is a blood source. So extra-uterine gestations are possible and have even occurred in male baboons (they would require a C-section-like delivery if brought to term).[6] So all the elements are in place for the next stage of in vitro fertilization. Adam and Steve will be little Johnnie's biological parents, birth parents, and parent parents. The Pennsylvania scientists assume that it is just a matter of time before they can coax stem cells from women to turn into sperm. Thomas Murray, president of the bioethics think-tank, the Hastings Center, says of the University of Pennsylvania study: "It will take a nanosecond for people in same-sex relationships to figure out the potential implications of this research for them. People can just fill in the blanks."[7]

* * *

If the popular and legal definitions of marriage, even ones that take procreation as the hidden determinate of marriage, all fail to give accounts of the content of marriage, what then is marriage after all? What is the content of the unions that count as marital?

Marriage is the development and maintenance of intimacy through the medium of everyday life, the day-to-day. To put it somewhat poetically, marriage is the fused intersection of love's sanctity and necessity's demand. It is the sanctity of love—love being a value for which one stands ready to make sacrifices—that places marriage on a par with a person's religious values, while it is the role of life's necessities in marriage that tethers marriage to nature, viewed not as a model for one's actions but as the very substrate of one's existence. You are married to someone when your love for that person—and their love for you—is grounded in and grows from the very means by which you jointly meet your basic needs—maintain a household and fulfill other everyday necessities. Life's necessities are a mixed fortune: on the one hand, they frequently are drag, dross, and cussedness, yet on the other hand, they can constitute opportunity, abidingness, and prospect for nurture. They are the field across which, the medium through which, and the ground from which the intimacies that we consider marital flourish, blossom, and come to fruition.

Not all loves or intimate relations count or should count as marriages. Culturally speaking, we are disinclined to think of Great Loves as marriages. Antony and Cleopatra, Tristan and Isolde, Catherine and Heathcliff—these are loves that burn gloriously but too intensely ever to be manifested in a medium of breakfasts and tire-changes. Nor are Americans inclined to consider as real marriages arranged marriages between heads of state who never see each other, for again the relations do not grow in the earth of day-to-day living.

Friendships too are intimate relations that we do not consider marital relations. Intimate relations are ones that acquire the character they have—that are unique—because of what the individuals in the relation bring to and make of it; the relation is a distinctive product of their separate individualities. Thus intimate relations differ markedly from public or commercial transactions, where, say, there is nothing distinctive about your sales clerk that bears on the meaning of your buying a pair of socks from him. The clerk is just carrying out a role, fulfilling a function, one that from the buyer's perspective nearly anyone could have carried out. Although friendships are star cases of intimate relationships, we do not count them as marriages; for while a person might count on a friend in a pinch to take her to the hospital, friendly relations do not usually manifest themselves through such necessities of life.

On the other hand, neither do we count roommates, even "domestic partners," who regularly cook, clean, tend to household chores, and share household finances as married, if all they do is "share the common necessities of life." Marriage requires the presence and blending of both necessity and intimacy.

The account of marriage I have given here is not revolutionary, it's quite traditional. Basically it is what common-law marriages are: a couple begins living intimately in a household of their own creation; they view themselves as living open-endedly this way and hold their relationship out to the public as an abiding blend of intimacy and the everyday. In the Anglo-American tradition, until the mid-nineteenth century this was in fact the most common form of marriage. Couples did not in general go to the state to secure a marriage license that marked and legally decreed them as married. Marriage was not dependent upon a state-run licensing scheme, though it came with all the legal incidents of a state-licensed, ceremonially solemnized marriage. Common-law marriages were acknowledged by the law but were not creatures of the law. It is important to note that the standard "seven year" rule applied to common-law marriages was an evidentiary rule, not a constitutive rule. After a couple had lived together for seven years, there was an irrebuttable presumption that the couple was married, but they were, for purposes of rights and obligations at law, viewed as married from the day they began living intimately in a jointly maintained household. So, for instance, children born in the second year of a common-law marriage were as legitimate as those born in the ninth.

From the late 1800s, the trend in American law has been for governments to arrogate to themselves the sole power to create legally acknowledged marriages and to eliminate legal recognition for common-law marriages. Still, into the twenty-first century, the District of Columbia and eleven states (Alabama, Colorado, Iowa, Kansas, Montana, Oklahoma, Pennsylvania, Rhode Island, South Carolina, Texas, and Utah) still acknowledge common-law marriages.[8] But the overall result of the legal trend against common-law marriage has been for people to forget what the *content* of marriage is, and to suppose that marriage is just whatever the law says it is.

Though, by my account, marriage is not, in the first instance, a creature of the state, the law does have a number of important roles to play in and around marriage. The main function of marital law is to support, enhance, and extend marriage understood in the primary sense that I have developed. And indeed the required blending of intimacy and the everyday within marriage explains the *form* that the legal struts that nest around marriage actually take.

Marital law promotes the patient caring that such life requires (by providing for privacy, nurture, mutual support, and persistence), and it protects against the occasions when necessity is cussed rather than opportune, especially when life is marked by changed circumstance—crisis, illness, and destruction.

First and foremost, marriage changes strangers-at-law into next-of-kin with all the rights that this status entails, including the right to enter hospitals, jails, and other places restricted to "immediate family," the right to obtain "family" health insurance and bereavement leave, the right to live in neighborhoods zoned "single family only," and the right to make medical decisions in the event a partner is injured or incapacitated.

Both from the partners themselves and from the state, marriage provides a variety of material supports that ameliorate, to a degree, necessity's unfriendly intervals. Marriage requires mutual support between spouses. This duty holds whether or not there are any children in the family. The legal obligation to care for one's children exists independent of marital law and is grounded separately from it.

Marriage provides income tax advantages, including deductions, credits, improved rates, and exemptions. It provides for enhanced public assistance in times of need. It governs the equitable control, division, acquisition, and disposition of community property. At death, it guarantees rights of inheritance in the absence of wills—a right of special benefit to the poor, who frequently die intestate. For the wealthy, marriage virtually eliminates inheritance taxes between spouses, since spouses as of 1981 can make unlimited untaxed gifts to each other even at death. For all, it exempts property from attachments resulting from one partner's debts. It confers a right to bring a wrongful death suit. And it confers the right to receive survivor's benefits.

Several marital benefits promote a couple's staying together in the face of changed circumstances. These include the right to collect unemployment benefits if one partner quits her job to move with her partner to a new location because the partner has obtained a new job there, and the right to obtain residency status for a noncitizen partner. Currently lesbian and gay couples are denied all of these rights in consequence of being barred access to legal marriages, even though these rights and benefits are as relevant to committed lesbian and gay relationships as to heterosexual marriages.

The blending of intimacy and everyday life in marriage also explains the legal privacy rights that inhere in the marital bond. Take one example: the immunity that spouses have against being compelled to testify against each other. Because marital relations are intimate, they can only thrive within a presumption of trust between partners, and yet because the relationship is woven through the details of everyday life, there will be a transparency of information between partners—they will know virtually everything about each other. One cannot develop trust if one has to worry constantly that everything about one's life might be hauled into the public eye. This pairing of trust and transparency within marriage constitutes the moral ground for the legal immunity against compelled testimony between spouses, and explains too why this immunity is not extended to (mere) friends. The spousal immunity against compelled testimony is waived when relations with one's own children are what is at legal stake, as in cases of alleged child abuse. This exception is another example showing that marital rights are not grounded in marriage's being thought of as an incubator for procreation.

In most jurisdictions, deciding the manner in which someone is to be buried is a statutory right of the next-of-kin—and so gay people are frequently barred by the deceased's kin from even attending the funeral of their partners. Here the injustice of the law rises to the level of cruelty in its blindness to lived values.

* * *

It used to be that the rights and obligations that nested around marriage, the legal institution of marriage (if you will), acknowledged gender differences within the marital union—by doling out roles, rights, and duties depending on which spouse was male, which female. But these gender differences have all been found to be unjust, and, while no one was really looking, the differences have gradually all been eliminated from marital law through either legislative or judicial means. It used to be that husbands had an obligation to take care of their wives' material needs without their wives (no matter how wealthy) having any corresponding obligation to look after their husbands (however poor). Now both spouses are mutually and equally obliged. It used to be that a husband could sell his wife's property without her consent. The wife had no independent power to make contracts. It used to be that a husband could *by definition* not rape his wife—one could as well rape oneself, the reasoning went. These past embarrassing incidents of traditional legal marriage are now gone. The "one *man* and one *woman*" entrance requirement for marriage is now a husk that is dead, dead, dead, no matter how tenaciously it still attaches to the legal institution of marriage.

Neither the content of marriage (viewed as a mode of day-to-day living) nor the legal form of marriage (viewed as a network of rights and obligations supporting and protecting that mode of living) requires spouses to be of different genders.

Current society and its discriminatory impulses make lesbian and gay coupling difficult. Still even against oppressive odds, gays and lesbians have shown an amazing tendency to nest. The portraits of lesbian and gay committed relationships that emerge from ethnographic studies—like Philip Blumstein and Pepper Schwartz's *American Couples*

(1983), David McWhirter and Andrew Mattison's *The Male Couple* (1984), Kath Weston's *Families We Choose* (1991), and Christopher Carrington's *No Place Like Home* (2002)—suggest that in the way they typically arrange their lives, gay and lesbian couples fulfill the primary definition of marriage in an exemplary manner.[9]

Because of the loosening of traditional gender roles within gay relationships, the ways in which the day-to-day demands of necessity are typically fulfilled within lesbian and gay relationships are particularly fine-grained as vehicles for the development of intimacy. It is true that gay and lesbian couples generally divide duties between the partners—this is the efficient thing to do, the very first among the economies of scale that coupledom affords. But who does what is a matter of personal preference and joint planning, rather than the result of gender expectations. Decisions are made in part with an eye to who is better at doing any given task and who has free time—say, for ironing or coping with car dealerships. But adjustments are made in cases where one person is better at most things—or even everything; here the relation is made less efficient for the sake of equality between partners, who willingly end up doing things they would rather not do—not out of a sense of traditionally assigned duty and role, but out of an impulse to help out, a willingness to sacrifice, and a commitment to equality. In these ways, both the development of intimacy through choice and the proper valuing of love are intricately interwoven in the day-to-day activities of lesbian and gay couples. Choice improves intimacy. It makes sacrifices meaningful. It gives love its proper weight.

Nongays and many gays too are mistaken to think that the sacred valuing of love is something that can be imported from the outside, in public ceremonies invoking praise from God or community. Even wedding vows can smack of cheap moral credit, since they are words not actions. The sacred valuing of love must come from within and realize itself over time through little sacrifices in day-to-day existence. In this way, intimacy takes on weight and shine, the ordinary becomes the vehicle of the extraordinary, and the development of the marital relation becomes a mirror reflecting eternity. It is more proper to think of weddings with their ceremonial trappings and invocations as joyous bon voyages offered for the hopefully splendid two-character story that is beginning, rather than as a social institution that, echoing the legal institution of marriage, defines and confers marital status. In a gay marriage, the sanctifications that descend instantly through custom and ritual in many heterosexual marriages, descend gradually over and through time—and in a way they are better for it. For the sacred values and loyal intimacies contained in a gay marriage are a product of the relation itself; they are truly the couple's own.

\* \* \*

Marriage, the social form, is an ever-evolving institution, not an eternal verity. In America, it seems nothing changes quite so much as tradition. In general, marriage and family law reform have been evolving ever more in the direction of justice. Inequitable distributions of power by gender have been eliminated as a legally enforced part of marriage. The shift over the last fifty years from universal at-fault divorce to no-fault divorce as the law of the land has severed marriage's former eerie similarities to indentured servitude. This continuous progress toward justice in family life makes me doubt the view of many lesbian social theorists and quite a number of nonlesbian feminists as well that legal marriage is too sexist, oppressive, and violent an institution ever to be salvaged.[10]

In the past and now, people at the margins of society have frequently provided the beacon for reform in family law. Already, by the 1930s, black American culture no longer stigmatized children born out of wedlock, though whites continued to do so. In 1972, the Supreme Court belatedly came to realize that punitively burdening innocent children is profoundly unjust, and subsequently through a series of some thirty Supreme Court cases, illegitimacy has all but vanished as a condition legally affecting children born out of wedlock.[11] Further, black Americans provided to the mainstream the model of the extended family with its major virtue of allowing families to have a certain amount of open texture and play at the joints. In 1977, this virtue too was given constitutional status when the Supreme Court struck down zoning laws that discriminated against extended, typically black, families.[12]

Gay life, like black culture, might also provide models and materials for rethinking and improving family life. I close this chapter by charting some ways in which this might be so—in some cases drawing on the distinctive experience and ideals of gay male couples. Many lesbian moral theorists have found all forms of coupledom to be suspect. Some recommend communal arrangements as the ideal for lesbians; others have proposed that lovers should not even live together. By contrast, I believe that America will see a dialectical development between—among—same-sex couples, different-sex couples, and other familial arrangements, a development in which each group will learn something from the others and all people will be the better for it no matter how they structure their particular relationships. Example: Gay marriage admittedly changes the crisp and concrete "bride and groom" entries on marriage licenses to the nebulous and leadenly bureaucratic "applicant 1 and applicant 2," but in doing so, it takes marriage a major step toward justice for transsexual and transgendered people. What is lost by way of romance is more than compensated for with goodness, and in any case, it's not a function of the state to provide romance. Brides and grooms can always double their lace purchases and stag parties if they want extra romance.

Elements of relationships that traditionally made coupledom suspect will be winnowed away in the dialectical process:

*Choice improves intimacy.* When straight couples give in to socially assigned gender roles as what determines the divisions of labor within marriage, their relationships are more like commercial transactions than friendships. They lose intimacy. Relationships become mere systems of interlocking functions rather than unique matrixes developed out of that which is special about each person and from the couple's ability to jointly make decisions. Relations are more intimate the more fine filamented their materials. So traditional gender roles are an impediment rather than a resource for intimacy. Straight couples might learn a thing or two along these lines by looking to the relationships of their gay and lesbian friends.

*Choice makes sacrifice meaningful. Choice gives love its proper weight.* Take sex. Traditionally, monogamy was an adjunct of property law, or a vehicle for guaranteeing succession, or a lasso with which society would try to break, tame, and manage the wild beast of desire—break, tame, and manage, one might add, for *its own* projects, not the projects of the individuals upon whom it imposed monogamy. If a person's sexual behavior is protected by a fundamental right, then all these functions of coerced monogamy are illegitimate. To condition access to marriage upon monogamy would be like conditioning access to marriage upon holding certain religious beliefs or belonging to a certain political party.

To the extent that monogamy had a possible legitimate function, it was a chief mode of sacrifice imposed upon married couples as a means for them to show their sacred valuing of their relation. But gay men have realized that while sexual sacrifices may well be part of the sacrifices that a couple choose to make in order to show and ratify their love for each other, it is not necessary for this purpose. There are many other ways to do that. Love would not be properly valued if the couple were unwilling to make any sacrifices for it. But the sacrifices need not be sexual ones. The scary news is that monogamy is not an essential component of love and marriage.

Further the actions that make up a sacrificial offering are significant as a means of investing value in the thing for which the sacrifice is made *only* if the actions are performed voluntarily. If you say adorational prayers to God only because someone has a gun pressed to your head, the prayers count for nothing, and God is not worshipped thereby. Paying taxes is not a form of patriotism. Volunteering to fight in a just war is. So enforced monogamy actually turns out to stand at odds with the value of marital intimacy—in two ways. As a compelled course of action, it fails to be a mode of honoring the relationship. And to the extent that it is externally imposed on the couple, not a choice the couple makes, it fails to be a development of their distinctive characters and capacities. It fails to make their relationship unique or special. It fails to meet the criteria of what an intimate relation is.

The authors of *The Male Couple* found that "the majority of [gay male] couples, and *all* of the couples together for longer than five years, were not continuously sexually exclusive with each other. Although many had long periods of sexual exclusivity, it was not the ongoing expectation for most. We found that gay men *expect* mutual emotional dependability with their partners [but also believe] that relationship fidelity transcends concerns about sexuality and exclusivity." The law should acknowledge this possibility more generally. Indeed, half the states have decriminalized adultery. And the nation, though it is unwilling to admit it, has already tacitly accepted the notion that compelled monogamy is not an essential component of marriage: when a certain white stain on a certain blue dress proved that a certain U.S. president had not been monogamous with his wife, no one presumed that this meant that their marriage was ended. The choice to be monogamous or not fell to them, not the state. The nation knows this, it just won't say so openly.

Other improvements that take their cue from gay male couplings might include a recognition that marriages as lived experience change over time, go through stages, evolve. The emphasis that the nation puts on marriage certificates and wedding ceremonies as suddenly creating marriages in their entirety and in a fixed form, a single unalterable package, has caused people to believe that marriages are the same throughout their course, the same after fifty years as on day one. Even your parents can tell you that that vision is a bill of goods. *The Male Couple* distinguishes six stages that gay couples typically pass through: blending (year one), nesting (years two and three), maintaining (years four and five), building (years six though ten), releasing (years eleven through twenty), and renewing (beyond twenty years). Relations initially submerge individuality and emphasize equality between partners, though the equality usually at first takes the form of complementarity rather than similarity. With the passage of years, individuality reemerges. Infatuation gives way to collaboration. The development of a foundational trust between the partners and a blending of finances and possessions, interestingly enough, occurs rather late on—typically after ten years. While the most important factor in keeping men together over the first ten years is finding compatibility, the most important factor for the second decade is a casting off of possessiveness, even as the men's lives become more entwined materially and by the traditions and rituals they have established.

That relations evolve makes the top-down model of the law as the creator of marital relations particularly inappropriate for human life. Currently at law, the only recognition that marriages change and gather moral weight with time, is the vesting of one spouse's (typically the wife's) interests in the other's Social Security benefits after ten years of marriage. More needs to be explored along these lines. For example, one spouse's guaranteed share of the other's inheritance might rise with the logging of years, rather than being the same traditionally fixed, one-third share, both on day one of the marriage and at its fiftieth anniversary.

In gay male relations, the relation itself frequently is experienced as a third element or "partner" over and above the two men. This third element frequently has a physical embodiment in a home, business, joint avocation, or companion animal, but also frequently consists of joint charitable, civil, political, or religious work. The third element of the relation both provides a focus for the partners and relieves some of the confining centripetal pressures frequently found in small families. Whether this might have legal implications deserves exploration—it certainly provides a useful model for small heterosexually headed families.

All long-term gay male relationships, *The Male Couple* reports, devise their own special ways of making the relations satisfying: "Their styles of relationship were developed without the aid of visible role models available to heterosexual couples." This strongly suggests that legal marriage ought not to draw a tight net of obligations around couples if their long-term happiness is part of the law's stake. The law ought rather to provide a ground in which relations can grow and change and recognize their own endings.

\* \* \*

Two men clutch each other; one is at the edge of life.

"In sickness and in health."

The other has sold the house to pay the medical bills, changed the hospital sheets himself, sacrificed even beyond the point where assistance could help.

"For richer for poorer."

They are married to each other in their own eyes, in God's eyes, in the eyes of their church and community—in every eye but the law's.

"For better for worse."

And so now, as the doctor unplugs the respirator, as the lovers' duet ends, the law will put the living lover through a hell for which not even his beloved's decay could have prepared his imagination.

"Till death us do part."

*Chapter 4*

# Equality

A student—distraught—slips into the office of her high school guidance counselor. The student thinks she might be a lesbian. It is dawning on her that she seems to like girls rather than boys. And someone has just called her a derogatory name. The counselor tries to console, advise—counsel—the student to the best of her ability, given available resources. She suggests that being a lesbian is not the end of the world, that she herself, for example, likes women. Buoyed by her success counseling this student and another gay male student, the counselor begins to mention her bisexuality to some of the school's faculty. In consequence, she is fired. After a decade bouncing around the courts, her case reaches the U.S. Supreme Court in 1985; but only two justices—half the number needed—even want to hear her case, which claims her rights to equal protection have been violated. And so the Court lets stand a ruling that allows Ohio to fire all its gay and lesbian school teachers on the basis of their sexual orientation alone. Two decades later, this state of legal affairs is unchanged.

This chapter examines how we ought to understand the elusive concept "equal" when used in the Constitution's cryptic, if moving, promise that "no person shall be denied the equal protection of the law." It explores the moral background of the country's century-old belief that governments, both state and federal, should not be allowed to discriminate and tries to determine whether the constitutional promise of equality should be extended to include the protection of lesbians and gay men—as it currently does not. The next chapter examines the country's more recent belief that the private sector (private employers, realtors, hotels, restaurants, insurance companies, and the like) should also be barred from discriminating against certain groups and explores whether legislation barring such discrimination should encompass gay men and lesbians.

The task of this chapter is not an easy one. It requires answering the contested questions: What do we mean by equality anyway? What counts as discrimination? Are lesbians and gay men relevantly like other minority groups—blacks, the Irish, women, Jews, the handicapped, Mormons, and others—traditionally thought deserving of protection from governmental discrimination? And for that matter, what is a "minority"?

I suggest that equality in a moral sense is at heart a principle that asserts individuals as having equal dignity or personhood. Rising to the level of a right, equality is the authoritative claim that a person will not be held in lesser regard—as having less worth—unless that lesser regard is warranted by something the person has (or has not) done. A person may be held in lower regard, even contempt, because of some action he performs (say, lying, thieving, murdering) or because of his failure to perform some duty (say, neglecting to pay his taxes or feed his kids). Such acts and omissions permit and warrant censure and punishment. But a person may not legitimately be held in lower regard because of some status he or she has, some group membership independent of any action that establishes the person as a member of the group.

Equality at its core does not merely hold that one should treat similar cases similarly, that people should have equal access to whatever (other) rights there are. This merely formal principle is a component of procedural justice, but it does not exhaust or even capture the core of equality. Indeed if this were all equality is, equality would not add anything to whatever other rights there are, for all it would entail is that a right or a law should be applied consistently in its own terms—whatever those terms are. If its terms draw distinctions between groups, then so would its consistent application.

As odd as it may sound at first hearing, equality also cannot only or essentially mean equality of opportunity, though talk of "equal opportunity" is quite entrenched in America's folk rhetoric of justice and even in its institutional titles. The chief federal agency for the enforcement of the 1964 Civil Rights Act, for example, is called the Equal Employment Opportunity Commission.

Equality means something more. Consider the following paradigmatic racist joke taken from Blanche Knott's *Truly Tasteless Jokes, II*: "What do you call a black millionaire physicist who's just won the Nobel Prize? Answer: Nigger!" Here the incongruity, which is the basis of the joke's supposed fun, is that while the joke's subject through his actions has achieved the pinnacle of socially measured success, still he is viewed as a lesser, even naturally debased, being. The joke turns on the presumed (white) listener's assumption that the person's race makes him in some crucial sense unequal—assigns him a status, a grade of existence, immeasurably lower than the average person, the listener, even though his accomplishments are infinitely higher.

The joke is revelatory for understanding equality. First, the structure of the joke's humiliating fun shows that equality cannot chiefly mean equality of opportunity. The person in the joke has availed himself of and realized opportunity as fully as anyone could. The joke's butt could not launch a suit against the joke's teller, or anyone else, claiming that he had been denied access to some right, some freedom, some opportunity—for he has it all. Rather the joke presumes that true equality is a consequence of one's status and has nothing to do with one's actions. In the joke's moral system, which is to say America's popular morality, this person could never be equal no matter what he did.

Second, the joke shows that the lesser status which inequality assigns its object is a devolution away from the standard of full personhood. Here, race eliminates the subject of the joke from being viewed fully as a person—that is, as an individual with ends of his own, the ability to revise those ends, and the ability to respect others as having ends of their own. The subject is viewed rather as at best an object, tool, or thing. In the social dynamics of this joke, the black person is merely an instrument for others' entertainment, like a porpoise at SeaWorld.

This same moral vision was espoused by the Supreme Court in 1856 when it upheld the moral acceptability of slavery, claiming that blacks are an "unfortunate race ... [correctly] regarded as being of an inferior order, and altogether unfit to associate with the white race, either in social or political relations; and so far inferior, that they had no rights which the white man was bound to respect; that the Negro might justly and lawfully be reduced to slavery for his own benefit."[1] Although slavery is, like a tax too high, an unjust restriction on liberty, the chief moral problem with slavery is that it is a violation of equality. An injury, a harm, or a restriction to one's freedom may interrupt one's ability to carry out one's life plan, but an assault on equality, viewed as individual dignity, presumes that one is not even the sort of thing to deserve the status of having a life plan in the first place. To be treated inequitably is to be held in morally lesser regard independent of what one has done. It is to suffer degradation and humiliation.

Now admittedly, dignity itself is an elusive notion, but it can be placed in a conceptual network that helps clarify its nature. Consider what counts as a harm or offense against dignity. The common phrase "adding insult to injury" affords an intuitive grasp of a distinction between two types of offense. An insult is an offense against dignity, while an injury is something that reduces one's happiness, denies one some benefit, wealth, power, or useful possession, or generally reduces one's material circumstances in the world.

This distinction between dignity and well-being or happiness is also reflected in the different moral emotions we feel toward those whose well-being or dignity is of interest to us. The moral emotion that has happiness and harm as its proper objects is sympathetic concern—sympathetic joy or sympathetic sorrow. But we feel sympathetic concern, even love, for things that are not full persons, for example, pets. In contrast, the appropriate moral feeling directed to another's dignity is not sympathy, but respect. If our regard for others does not include respect, we fail to treat them as persons, and treat them instead as lesser beings.

Insults are a graver form of evil than injuries, for they attack persons as persons—in two ways. First, by focusing importance on largely irrelevant characteristics, insults treat the insulted as though their moral agency counts for nothing. Thus raw invectives, like "nigger" and "faggot," violate their targets' right to equal respect in that the insulted person's ability to formulate and carry out a plan of life—to realize his desires, plans, aspirations, and sense of the sacred—is not considered worthy of social care and concern on a par with that of others.

Second, by holding a person in morally diminished regard, insults also show disrespect for persons by treating those insulted as though they were not really full moral agents to begin with. In this way, metaphor-inflected invective (say, calling a black adult male "boy" or "buck" or a woman "babe," "girl," "bitch," or "cow") demotes the insulted person to the level of children or nonhuman animals, creatures who are not held responsible for their actions, who are not viewed as creators of their own destinies, and who require paternalistic intervention for their own good.

\* \* \*

The ill-treatment of gay men and lesbians chiefly takes the form of denials of equality. To be sure, lesbians and gay men are subject to violations of freedom and inflictions of severe harms. Still, these violations and inflictions are usually perpetrated with an eye to their serving as vehicles for the denial of equality. Being fired or being physically attacked because one is gay is a harm, but even more so it is a degradation. In cracking the skull of one gay man, the queerbasher is looking to insult all gay men, by framing all gay men as being death-worthy for who they are. The particular victim is a stand-in for the whole group. Gay oppression is chiefly the denial of gay dignity.

A detailed look at language will perhaps provide the most telling complex of examples to show that gays in America are indeed viewed—and, in turn, treated—inequitably as a group degraded independent of any behavior that makes one a member of the group.

Surprisingly, even nonslang terms used to denote gay men and lesbians preponderantly indicate that society does not think of homosexuals as defined by certain kinds of acts. Dictionaries' trackings of common usage and their definitions of "homosexual" reveal much, especially ones from the era before the gay rights movement made the term "homosexual" a contested one. The *Oxford English Dictionary* (1964) defines "homosexual" simply and solely as "having a sexual propensity for persons of one's own sex." Similarly *Webster's New Twentieth Century* (1952) has for the adjective "characterized by sexual inclination toward the same sex," and for the noun "one whose emotions, feelings, and desires are concerned with the individual's own sex rather than with the opposite sex." No mention of actions is made here. Actions are not necessary for the label to apply to a person. Nor, importantly, are actions here even sufficient for the label to apply. For one can, and quite often does, will and perform actions without having a desire, inclination, propensity, or (positive) feeling for the actions performed—carrying out arduous tasks and undergoing major surgery are actions of this sort.

Antigay slurs in American English also target a person's status rather than behavior. With the apparent exception of "cocksucker," no widespread antigay slur gives any indication that its censure is directed at sex acts rather than despised social status. Group-directed slurs (dyke, queer, fag) place lesbians and gay men in a significant social category along with blacks (nigger, shine, shitskin), other racial groups (chink), women (cunt, gash), various ethnic groups (wop, dago, gook, jap, JAP, mick, kike), religious groups (kike, papist, christer), native peoples (redskin, injun, Eskimo), nonnative peoples (kike, gypsy), and the physically challenged (crip, gimp, veg, vegetable, crispy critter). It does not place them in the same category as liars, hypocrites, murderers, and thieves—those who commit immoral and criminal actions and yet for whom culture in no case has coined group-based invectives. This schema of slurs strongly suggests that gay men and lesbians are held to be immoral because they are hated, rather than hated because they are immoral.

What of "cocksucker"? The slur is an example of what I call "moral retro-fitting." Though the term at first seems clearly to name a sex act and so might well seem to have behavior, not status, as the target of its derision, on analysis the term turns out to be used exclusively as a marker or placeholder for status. For the charge "cocksucker" has as little to do with sucking cock as the charge "motherfucker" has to do with fucking one's mother. "Cocksucker" stands to male homosexuality as "mackerel-eater" stands to Catholicism. In both cases, the name of an action (sucking, eating) is used as code for a status. We know this because "cocksucker" is never used as an aspersion cast against women who suck cock, just as "mackerel-eater" is never used against Protestants who happen to eat mackerel.

Many slang pejoratives explicitly denote homosexual status rather than homosexual acts. The whole host of put-downs of gay men nominally based on charges of effeminacy are of this sort. They put down gay men not as performers of sodomy but as having a low status derivative from the low status in which society holds women, and additionally from the sense that they have betrayed their socially assigned gender-status. To be sure, betrayal is a willful action, but here it is not the willfulness of being a "queen" that is the brunt of slurs like "sissy" and "nelly." It is the challenge that the queen's status presents to socially managed gender distinctions that is condemned. Hence the condemnation of will is inextricably bound up with the protection of status—the queen's very existence is a challenge to the status "real manhood." Action has little to do with the perceived threat.

A useful probe for determining whether a complex social classification, like effeminacy, has been made purely with respect to actions or whether references to actions are being morally retrofitted and used as markers of status is to imagine whether for the class one could draw up criteria that capture the individuals of the class one by one, without first treating the class as a social grouping and only then being able to pick out its members. Take hippies, for example. For every action that one might think definitive of a hippie (smoking pot, wearing "weird" clothes, being given to love, loafing, etc.), one can find some other group that performs that action, but which is not put down as a group by reference to that particular action—yuppies do drugs; supermodels frequently wear weird clothes; Christians are given to love, fishing buddies to loaf. What (middle-class) society didn't like about hippies was the whole package, their whole complex of attitudes and behaviors, which itself could never pass muster for assigning, say, individual criminal accountability. So even though being a hippie, like being a member of a religion, is a matter of choice, still hippies were despised not as failed moral agents but as bearers of a degenerate status. The Supreme Court acknowledged this in 1973 with a decision holding that a household could not be denied food stamps on the grounds that it contained members whom the government thought were hippies.[2]

Similarly, with effeminacy in gay men and butchness in lesbians, they are each, like being a hippie, a complex characteristic that cannot be given a clear enough characterization to be counted as a culpable action, and such actions as are part of the makeup of each do not have enough independent life to justify moral censure of them. The component parts of the status—say, a limp wrist and a swinging gait or wearing flannel and smoking stogies—are distinctively and immediately despised not on their own as possibly blameworthy acts but because they, like "hippie behavior," are signs or markers for a despised status. What the effeminate male or butch lesbian *does* does not matter. It is their mere existence, mere presence, that offends. Such acts as homosexuals are thought to perform—whether sexual, gestural, or social—are viewed socially as the expected or even necessary effluvia of homosexuals' lesser moral state, of their status as lesser beings, rather than as the distinguishing marks by which they are defined as a group.

Such purported acts—the stuff of stereotypes—provide the materials for a retrospectively constructed ideology concocted to justify the group's despised status, just as, for instance, beliefs that Jews poison wells and kill babies and messiahs are concocted, as socially "needed," to justify society's hatred of Jews. Hatred's targeting of status is primitive, and its condemnation of behavior an ideologically inspired afterthought.

Another large set of slurs explicitly denote status in their metaphoric vehicles and thus suggest that their target—male homosexuality—is also being viewed as a status. These slurs include: pansy, panz, fruit, fruitcake, and *finocchio* (Italian for fennel and the name of a decades-old Sausalito transvestite bar). These slurs, which have no lesbian counterparts, obviously make no reference to behavior of any kind. All of them derive from the cosmic order "vegetable," and vegetables don't do anything.

These slurs suggest that America's mind believes in a Great Chain of Moral Being. Straight men—fully real persons—constitute the highest tier of all the gradations of human moral worth. Of sublunar beings, they are nearest the ascending heavenly hierarchy of saints, cherubim, seraphim, archangels, and gods. Descending down the chain from real men, we arrive next at women, whose nature is essentially, abidingly, and pervasively viewed in slang as animal. Women are chiefly referred to in slurs by designations of animal species (bitch, beaver, cow, fish, vixen, pussy, shrew), by terms which assimilate women to immature animals and children (chick, doll, babe, baby, girl), or which reduce women to the body parts by which their animality differs from that of males (cunt, gash, beaver, pussy, bag, muff, rack). Note that there are no corresponding derogatory terms for males in contemporary culture. The derogatory terms that have male genitalia as their metaphoric vehicles—prick, dick, dickhead—are not in fact putdowns of men as men, but are simply equivalents to "bozo," "dolt," or "jerk." Real men are unassailable. Their antipode down at the bottom of the human heap is vegetable existence—pansies, fruits, *and* the physically challenged, who, like gay men, also are typically denoted and demoted with vegetative slurs. The lowly placement of gay men on a scale that contains women, men, and the congenitally deformed shows that the social treatment of gay men depends not upon what they do but upon some perceived degenerate status.

Quite generally then, it would appear that when animosity against some group reaches a level where the group is the subject of highly developed, sharply derisive slang and the butt of vicious jokes, then the group's members are being held accountable not for what they do, but for what they are. At present society chooses to treat gay men and lesbians not as agents of their own destiny, but simply as having a degenerate status for which questions of action and accountability are irrelevant.

In addition to the linguistic record, much more and diverse evidence shows that in lopsided preponderance, society views lesbians and gay men first and foremost as morally lesser beings. In the 1980s three major institutions—the military, religion, and medicine—

weighed in to affirm the moral model that classifies lesbians and gay men by status rather than actions.

*The military:* According to the formulations developed in the early 1980s to carry out the military's ban on homosexuals, it turns out that engaging in homosexual behavior is neither a necessary nor a sufficient condition for being considered a homosexual and treated accordingly. In these formulations, homosexual desire (as expressed, say, in a diary entry) is, even in the absence of any behavior, sufficient to have one kicked out of the armed forces for being homosexual; yet if a member of the armed forces is caught actually performing homosexual acts, he is permitted to plead successfully that these do not indicate his true nature and that "such conduct is a departure from the member's usual and customary behavior." One may claim, "Just skylarking," or "Boy, was I drunk last night," and be retained. Clearly in these formulations, it is one's status as a homosexual—a status that can float completely separate from any behavior—that is the brunt of military policy.

*Religion:* In 1986, the Catholic church, in a major ideological shift, branded as "an objective moral disorder" the mere status of being a homosexual, even when congenitally fixed and unaccompanied by any homosexual behavior. Previously, such status had been viewed as morally neutral and only homosexual acts—sins—were morally censured. Both the Vatican letter stating this shift, a 1992 Vatican letter interpreting it as warranting employment discrimination against lesbians and gay men, and a Vatican letter of 2003 saying that the mere presence of gay people constitutes violence against children, all seemed, by their wording and the way they framed issues, to be a specific response to the development of lesbian and gay politics in the United States.[3] Political stirring produced ideological retrenchment, in a way, though, that tipped religion's hand. The Catholic church's conception of gay people is a species of racism.

*Medicine:* On April 15, 1985, in Atlanta, during the keynote address for the first International Conference on AIDS, President Reagan's secretary of health and human services, Margaret Heckler, in a burst of good intentions gone painfully awry, held: "We must conquer AIDS before it affects the heterosexual population ... the general population. We have a very strong public interest in stopping AIDS before it spreads outside the risk groups, before it becomes an overwhelming problem."[4] The determinate prospect of a million or so dead gay men was not seen to be a problem for the Reagan administration. Now, in America the value of a person's life is not normally pegged by reference to the means by which the person comes to have diseases. For instance, the life of a CEO who suffers a heart attack from years of gluttony is not thought to be worth less than that of a person who suffers a heart attack under torture. So that even if one drew a moral distinction between the HIV-conveying sex acts of heterosexuals and those of homosexuals, still this would not ground a further distinction between lives to be saved and lives to be junked. So it is not the moral assessment of actions that grounds Heckler's distinction; rather she holds heterosexual status as more worthy of care and concern than gay men's status. Gays, here, are lesser beings; their agency doesn't matter.

The social understanding of homosexuality essentially as a degenerate status rather than as a form of censurable behavior was given its clearest and most honest formulation in the twentieth century by Heinrich Himmler, who, in a speech to his SS generals, explained that the medieval German practice of drowning male homosexuals in bogs "was no punishment, merely the extermination of an abnormal life. It had to be removed just as we [now] pull up stinging nettles, toss them on a heap, and burn them."[5]

\* \* \*

Society's conceptualization of lesbians and gay men as possessing a degenerate status has important consequences for understanding gay men and lesbians as a minority. In its most central, frequent and important usage, "minority" is a normative rather than a descriptive term. Rare is its use in its descriptive, statistical meaning—"less than 50 percent"—as in "the bill failed to pass because it garnered only a minority of the legislators' votes."

Perhaps surprisingly, "minority" in its normative sense does not even entail the term's descriptive or statistical sense. The expression now found in job advertisements encouraging "women and other minorities to apply" and in past federal set-aside programs that counted women as a minority shows that the statistical sense of "minority" is not a necessary condition for the correct application of the term taken in its normative sense.

On what then does "being a minority" turn? I think the American military, American English, the Catholic church, and Margaret Heckler provide a sufficient clue. A minority is a group treated unjustly because of some status that the group is socially perceived to possess independent of the behavior of the group's members. A "minority" is a group whose members have been treated inequitably. This definition captures the scope and normative force of the term. Thus it is that women, though statistically a majority, are considered a minority, whereas people with blue eyes, though statistically a minority, are not: there are no minority set-aside programs for people with blue eyes. Yet, given this definition, current discussions of gay and lesbian people as a minority have been largely misguided because irrelevant.

Almost all the popular debate about gay men and lesbians—and a fair amount of the academic debate—has turned on whether being gay is an immutable characteristic, a property that the gay person cannot change. If it is, gay men and lesbians would be, so it is claimed, relevantly like blacks—like, in that one's group characteristic is not of one's own doing, with the result that in a group-based discrimination one is treated unjustly because treated without regard to what one oneself has done. But even if it were conclusively proven that being homosexual is not a matter of choice, we would still have to be careful in drawing conclusions from that fact. For sometimes making social distinctions with respect to nonchosen properties is morally acceptable, even morally to be expected. For example, "grandfathering provisions" are not, in themselves, considered unjust. A law with a grandfathering provision blocks future access to a privilege but allows those currently granted the privilege to maintain it (say, a vendor's license or a land use at odds with newly restrictive zoning). If grandfather exceptions do not front for some illegitimate goal (for example, perpetuating racial oppression in the post-Reconstruction era), then they are not felt to be substantially unjust, even though they create closed classes of people with privileges to which others, sometimes simply as a matter of when they were born, can have no access no matter what they do. Or again:

a law that lowers the inheritance tax rate will disadvantage a person whose parents have already died compared to people whose parents have not yet died. Still this disadvantage is not an injustice to him, even though its falling upon him is not a consequence of anything he has done. All sorts of legitimate state programs and laws give different people differential access to certain opportunities, but this does not automatically mean that they constitute violations of a fundamental right.

When taken as a moral principle, the claim that one is not to be discriminated against with respect to some characteristic over which one has no control has all the usefulness but roughness of a rule of thumb—immutable characteristics *usually* will be morally irrelevant. If a law makes a distinction with reference to an immutable characteristic, it deserves a close second look to make sure that people's immutable characteristics are not being given a moral weight they do not warrant and that the law's distinction-drawing indeed advances a legitimate government project. But barring that, and as long as the law does not degrade some group, it is morally acceptable. Immutable characteristics are not sufficient conditions for triggering minority status and minority protections.

Neither are immutable characteristics necessary conditions for moral minority status. Among minorities that have properly invoked constitutional protections are religious minorities and the physically challenged *even* when the challenge in question is the result of actions for which the handicapped person himself is responsible, such as negligent driving or a botched suicide. Minority standing that is based only on biological or psychological determinism lets in both too much and too little.

Whether gays and lesbians are or are not in the eye of nature objectively like a highly distinctive ethnic group, that is how society views and treats them—as a despised ethnic minority and not as a pack of criminals. Society's attitudes toward and treatment of lesbians and gay men, as revealed in its treatment of them in slang and invective, derogatory group-based jokes, stereotypes, group-directed violence, the long existence of highly symbolic but virtually never enforced sodomy laws, Catholic theology, and health policy, all presuppose and reinforce the moral vision that lesbians and gay men are lesser moral beings.

This treatment justifies the application to gay people of the moral sense of minority, and in turn ought to invoke the constitutional norms the culture thinks appropriate for minority status, especially enhanced constitutional equal protections of the sort currently afford- ed by the Supreme Court to blacks, ethnic minorities, religious mi- norities, legal aliens, illegal alien children, illegitimate children, women, and the mentally and physically challenged.[6] For the treat- ment of lesbians and gay men corrupts both the substance and proce- dures of a constitutionally restrained democracy.

The social degradation of homosexuals and the existence of antigay stereotypes, for example, show that the concerns of lesbians and gay men individually are not *substantively* given equal care and concern with the concerns of members of the dominant culture. The needs, de- sires, and aspirations of gay men and lesbians simply do not command the respect of those who make up the majority and so either do not register at all or are devalued in the calculus effected by majority rule in its establishment of social policy. This reason alone is sufficient to show that lesbians and gay men need and deserve constitutional pro- tection from majoritarian decision-making.

Equally important though: society's treatment of gay men and les- bians tends to short-circuit the standard *procedures* of intelligent pub- lic policy-making and of justice more generally. Stereotypes and (other) hostile attitudes toward gay men and lesbians are not so much the effects of misperceiving gays and lesbians, of getting lesbians and gays wrong, but more so are what causes the misperception of them, and in turn the mistreatment of them. Antigay stereotypes and the like are not simply illegitimate as factual bases for making social decisions about lesbians and gay men, rather they are also lenses through which lesbian and gay people are viewed and assessed. Stereotypes become part of a person's cognitive capacities and evaluative apparatus, and so cause misjudgments, with both prejudicial treatment and social ineffi- ciency as their result. Because people are not aware, indeed frequently deny, that they have these judgment-distorting social lenses in their minds, they are frequently prejudiced without intending to be or even knowing that they are prejudiced. This social fact is extremely impor- tant for courts and government administrators to acknowledge, for it greatly distorts hiring decisions and fairness in the administration of criminal and civil justice.

Quite apart from any history of intentional discrimination against gay men and lesbians, the existence of antigay stereotypes operating as unacknowledged social lenses in policy-making insures that democratic processes cannot be relied upon to insure fair and impartial treatment of gay and lesbian concerns. Indeed the effects of stereotypes in society's judgment-making undercut the very grounds for affirming representational democracy as a form of government. When stereotypes are rife in culture, representative democracy cannot justify its policies as being the product of rational deliberation. For reasons of the coherence of democratic theory, gays and lesbians ought to be given enhanced equal protections against discrimination by government.

To put it bluntly: if the Supreme Court, which is structurally positioned to be above the fray of politics, can admit that it itself has been unable to give gay men and lesbians a fair shake—as it admits in *Lawrence v. Texas*'s recantation of *Bowers v. Hardwick*—then it would be irrational for the Court to assume that the fray of politics itself can give gay men and lesbians a fair shake. If the Court's redemptive reading of itself in *Lawrence* is not to ring as just so much hollow self-congratulations, the Court must now begin to move aggressively to address the remaining areas of law where distinctions are drawn with reference to sexual orientation.

\* \* \*

How does this model of equality play out in assessing whether specific laws are inequitable? A law will be a violation of equality if in its drafting it draws upon or in its effects enhances the view that some group is held in morally lesser regard independent of any action that puts a member of the group in the group. A law does not violate equality simply by virtue of its distributing some benefit or opportunity differently between two groups. As important: nor will the law necessarily be an equitable treatment in virtue of its distributing the same benefits and opportunities to different groups.

A differential distribution violates equality only if the distribution draws on or enhances society's perception that one of the groups is worthy of less moral regard than the other. So, for example, an affirmative action program that gives some benefits and opportunities to blacks that it does not give to whites would be inequitable only if the differential distribution would be socially read as deriving from or reinforcing social structures that hold white people in lesser moral regard than blacks—an impossibility in current American culture.

On the other hand, an identical distribution will be inequitable if it socially serves as a means of insulting, humiliating, or degrading one of the groups. Such is the case in most separate-but-equal schemes.

To determine whether a distribution insults or degrades a group, one has to look at the social context of the distribution. In some societies, a flicked middle finger might be a serious insult; in others it might be a meaningless gesture; in still others it might be a sign of greeting. More specifically, whether the flicked finger is an insult depends on how the culture *reads* the symbolism of the gesture. It does not turn on whether the target of the gesture reads it as an insult. Indeed the target need not even know that he has been insulted—he can be insulted nonetheless. Thus we say that a person can be insulted behind her back or even beyond the grave.

The Supreme Court got this all backward in the 1896 case *Plessy v. Ferguson* with which "separate but equal" was established as the law of land for more than half a century. The Court was wrong, almost certainly disingenuous, when it claimed that if blacks were insulted by being forced to sit in racially segregated railway coaches, the insult was the result of blacks' sensitivities not of the Louisiana law mandating the segregation.[7] The Louisiana legislature knew how the segregation would be socially read and the law was passed for that very reason. This segregation, like antimiscegenation laws, gave blacks and whites the same opportunities—blacks could not marry whites or sit in their coaches, whites could not marry blacks or sit in their coaches—but such identical treatments were inequitable because, socially viewed, the identical distributions were still means of society viewing blacks in lower social regard than whites. So the Supreme Court correctly ruled in 1967, when it finally declared antimiscegenation laws unconstitutional violations of equality.[8]

Now consider states like Vermont which have established licensing schemes that give homosexual couples exactly the same benefits and opportunities as they give heterosexual couples—except for the name "marriage" on the licenses issued to secure the rights and benefits. The licenses for gay and lesbian couples instead have "civil union" written on them. Is this licensing scheme an equitable treatment of gay men and lesbians?

It would not be an equitable treatment of lesbians and gay men, even if it were to give *more* privileges and benefits to them than to heterosexuals, just as it would still be inequitable to require blacks to sit at the back of a bus even if the bus had a "rear exit only" requirement that gave blacks the opportunity to exit the bus out the back door first. The reason is that the culture reads the ritual of placing blacks at the back of the bus as degrading to blacks.

So too, reserving the sacred sign "marriage" for heterosexuals when homosexuals are offered separate-but-equal civil unions, serves—and *only* serves—to degrade gay men and lesbians by denying them one of the chief social forms by access to which America marks out membership in full humanity. It is not just a word that is at stake, it is a highly symbolic civic ritual that civil union schemes deny gay men and lesbians. And the more politicians of all stripes call the *institution* of marriage itself sacred, rather than the love within a marriage or the couple's sacred valuing of their relationship, the more inequitable the separate-but-equal scheme becomes.

In December 2003, the Massachusetts legislature asked Massachusetts's highest court whether a civil-union arrangement that gave lesbian and gay couples all the rights and benefits of marriage, only just not the name "marriage," would meet the standard for equal treatment laid out in the court's November 2003 decision giving gay and lesbian couples the right to marry. By a four-to-three vote the court answered, "no."[9] To the bewilderment of the dissenting judges, the court clarified that, as far as equality was concerned, the civil union scheme was a more inequitable treatment of gay and lesbian couples than the state's past refusals to grant them marriage licenses, despite all the goodies that come along with civil union status, goodies that lesbian and gay couples did not have under the state's marriage laws. The

reason: The state's past refusal to give marriage licenses to gay and lesbian couples was based on a statute that, when it was drawn into
Massachusetts law from the English common law in 1810, was not established with lesbians and gay men in mind. The Massachusetts marriage law did not intentionally draw distinctions on the basis of sexual
orientation. By contrast, the civil union scheme was *intentionally*
drawn to distinguish heterosexuals from gays, and since all the rights
and obligations of unions and marriages would be the same under the
scheme, the distinction was *wholly* drawn to differentiate gays from
heterosexuals. The differentiation itself is one thick with social significance: "The [civil unions] bill would have the effect of maintaining
and fostering a stigma of exclusion that the Constitution prohibits. It
would deny to same sex 'spouses' only a status that is specially recognized in society and has significant social and other advantages. The
Massachusetts Constitution does not permit such invidious discrimination, no matter how well intended."

* * *

All this is true, but one could press even further. The law (it will be re-
membered) claims—and so does any society that accepts the law's
claim—that marriage is the only legally acknowledged relation between the sexes. Through marriage the law *creates* the legal relation between the sexes; the law, in short, *creates* heterosexuality legally speaking. Without legal marriage the sexes would be as related to each other
at law as mangos and tangos. Marriage more generally—religious, social, as well as, legal marriage—needs to be understood as an institution in current society that creates a social status, in particular heterosexual status—and then ratifies that status. Marriage—the legal and
social ritual—doesn't lay value on something that already exists. It
draws into being a social form, even as it ratifies that very form.
Marriage, in short, is an initiation ritual. A typical initiation ritual
takes a male and turns him into a man. Biology and nonritualistic behavior could not do that. So too biology and nonritualistic behavior
could not turn a person into a heterosexual. Indeed Don Juan,
Casanova, and Lothario, those frisky male seducers of endlessly nu-

merous ladies, are now taken as cultural symbols for homosexual denial rather than heterosexual affirmation. Not biology, not behavior, rather marital status is the social essence of heterosexuality. And the required ritual of marriage, getting wed—the legally, socially, religiously required ceremony of solemnization—is the initiation rite that both confers that status and endues it with value.

So the social and political stakes in marriage turn out to be much higher than even the Massachusetts court realized. It is not just any old nonmaterial benefit that gays and lesbians are being denied by civil union schemes, important as such nonmaterial benefit may be, say, access in a theater to the even-numbered seats that are thought to be particularly dear to the gods, even though the view of the stage is just a good from the odd-numbered seats. Rather in civil union schemes, all the sanctity and holiness associated with *heterosexual status per se* as created and ratified by the ritualistic solemnizing of marriages would be denied gays and lesbians *by law*. And more even than that, as intentionally and wholly designed to symbolically differentiate heterosexuals from gays around the very institution that in the eyes of the law and society heterosexuality is established, the separate-but-equal civil union scheme flags to society that to let lesbians and gays marry would be not just to besmirch the sanctity of heterosexuality, but more so to destroy heterosexuality itself. Analogously, if a colonial ruler imposed a new order of equality mandating that henceforth both males and females must go through the initiation rituals of manhood, then for those upon whom the new order is imposed, the new order would destroy manhood, would destroy what it is to be a man.

Civil union schemes then are instruments in the institutionalization of heterosexual supremacy just as, in the racist's mind, letting a black man marry a white woman would not just besmirch whiteness, but would also destroy the very ritual, pure-blood marriage, by which Caucasians are initiated into whiteness, are made white, and so further would destroy whiteness itself, what it means to be white. The parallels here between gays' justice and blacks' is more uncanny than even most lesbian and gay activists realize. In 1967, when the Supreme Court ruled antimiscegenation laws unconstitutional violations of equality, it did so on the ground that such laws were "measures designed to maintain White Supremacy." A future Court should declare civil-union schemes violations of equality on the ground that they are measures designed to create and maintain Heterosexual Supremacy.

It goes almost without saying that the enormous political resistance to gay marriage lies in the masses' conception of themselves as heterosexual. If gays could get married, heterosexuals would no longer be Heterosexuals. They would just be people. Horrors.

* * *

The natural human response to injuries is to direct at the source of the injuries the form of anger that is being riled up. Proper remedies are compensation and perhaps retribution. The natural human response to the source of insults that one suffers is not being riled up, but resentment, indignation, even righteousness—an anger that does not lash out in retaliation, but a pure, cool anger. The remedy sought cannot be compensation, for though one person can treat another as less than a person, one person cannot constitute another person as a moral agent with dignity. The proper action of the offended party is one that directly reasserts the dignity that was denied—for example, by publicly naming an insult as bigotry—in order to assert dignity in such a way that it cannot as easily be denied again, even if the person who thus asserts her dignity, by doing so, places herself at risk for harms, say, from a bigoted employer, police officer, or even a friend.

At the level of individual interactions, the goal of such assertion is heartfelt apology from the offender. In America there is a forum for the redress of those assaults to dignity that are perpetrated by government—the courts as expounders of constitutional rights, especially rights to equal protection. To the extent that antigay laws are an assault on dignity and to the extent that dignity is not, as it is not, something that ought morally to depend on the whims of majorities, then the courts are not just an available forum to overturn antigay discrimination, they are also the most appropriate forum. Given the inherently political nature of representative bodies, there is no effective equivalent on the social level to an individual's heartfelt apology. There is only the assertion of rights.

# Chapter 5
# Civil Rights

C urrent federal civil rights law bars private-sector discrimination in housing, employment, and public accommodations on the basis of race, national origin, ethnicity, gender, religion, age, and disability, but not sexual orientation. Where city councils and state legislatures have passed protections for gay men and lesbians, the protections have been under concerted and frequently successful attack through referendum initiatives. In 1997 and again in 2000, Maine's legislature passed statewide civil rights laws protecting gay men and lesbians only to have the law in each case overturned by referenda. This chapter offers moral arguments for protecting lesbians and gay men from private-sector discrimination.

The federal courts, including the Supreme Court, have over the last two decades regularly been cutting back on the scope and nature of protections that civil rights laws afford to groups already covered by federal and state statutes—by limiting remedies, limiting who has standing to bring suits, limiting the definition of what counts as discrimination, and even declaring some statutes unconstitutional under the court's emerging federalism—states' rights—doctrines and, in the case of discrimination by the Boy Scouts, under the First Amendment.[1]

The gay scout case is particularly disturbing for it lays down a line of thought along which all civil rights laws could easily be declared unconstitutional. The case held that the Boy Scouts' firing of a gay employee had an expressive content. It made a political point, and so was protected by freedom of speech. But speech rights and political rights are in the first instance possessed by individuals and only secondarily, or perhaps even derivatively, by groups. In any event, if a group's firing someone counts as expression covered by the First Amendment, then to an even greater extent an individual's firing someone would also be covered. As the decision was written, there is nothing distinctive about gay men and lesbians that limited the case's holding to them. Clearly by the case's lights, the Boy Scouts get to fire atheists as well. The case did not even consider the state's possible interests in passing civil rights laws or particular groups' interests in having such laws apply to them. So a reassessment of the values motivating civil rights legislation in general is in order, along with considerations of the particular interests gay men and lesbians have in acquiring such protections.

\* \* \*

Even though civil rights legislation restricts somewhat the workings of free enterprise, it promotes other core American values that far outweigh the slight loss of entrepreneurial freedom. These values are self-respect, self-sufficiency, general prosperity, and individual flourishing.

No one in American society can have much self-respect or maintain a solid sense of self if she is, in major ways affecting herself, subject to whimsical and arbitrary actions of others. Work, entertainment, and housing are major modes through which people identify themselves to themselves. Indeed in modern culture, work and housing rank just after personal relationships and perhaps (for some) religion, as the chief means by which people identify themselves to themselves. A large but largely unrecognized part of the misery of unemployment is not merely poverty and social embarrassment, but also a sense of loss of that by which a person defined herself, a loss that many people also experience upon retirement, even when their income and social esteem are left intact. People thrown out of work frequently compare this loss to the loss of a family member, especially to the loss of a child. Here the comparison is not simply to the intensity of the emotion caused by the loss, but to the nature of the loss: what was lost was a central means by which one constituted one's image of oneself.

Work is also a chief means by which people in America identify themselves to others. Indeed in America, a person's job is tantamount to his or her social identity. Socially one finds out who people are by finding out what they do. At social gatherings, like parties, asking after a person's employment is typically the first substantive inquiry one makes of a person to whom one has been introduced. America is a nation of doers. When job discrimination is directed at lesbians and gay men, say, as child-care workers or museum directors, it is a way of branding them as essentially un-American, as alien. It is a chief mode of expatriation from the national experience.

Discrimination in housing similarly affects a person's social identity. The physical separation of a group and its concentration apart from the dominant social order are among the chief means by which a group is socially marked as worthy of less respect, as unclean, as threatening. Housing discrimination against a despised group is apartheid writ small, but not small enough to be morally acceptable.

Discrimination in housing also affects a person's self-perception. It perhaps goes without saying that the conversion of a house into a home is one of the main facets of self-definition. Blocking or arbitrarily restricting the material basis of this conversion inhibits the development of self-respect and selectively disrupts the sanctities of private life. The common expression "keeping up with the Joneses," even in its mild censure or irony, attests to the role of housing in the way people identify themselves to themselves, in part, through the eyes of others. To be denied housing on the basis of some group status is another chief mode of social ostracism and exile.

In a nonsocialist, noncommunist society like America, there is a general expectation that each person is primarily responsible for meeting his or her own basic needs and that the government becomes an active provider only when all else fails. It is largely noncontroversial that people ought to have their basic needs met. For meeting basic needs is a necessary condition for anyone's being able to carry out a life plan. If government aims at enhancing the conditions in which people are able to carry out their life plans, then enhancing the conditions in which basic needs are met will be a high government priority, all the more so if the means to this end themselves intrude only slightly into life plans of others—employers and realtors who wish to discriminate.

Current civil rights legislation tries to unclog channels between an individual's efforts and the fulfillment of the individual's needs. For it is chiefly through employment, in conjunction with access to certain public accommodations and housing, that people acquire the things they need to assure their continued biological existence—food, shelter, and clothing. Importantly, these are also the chief means by which people acquire those various culturally relative needs that maintain them as credible players in the ongoing social, political, and economic "games" of the society into which they are born—say, needs for transportation and access to information. Civil rights legislation, then, helps people discharge their presumptive obligation to meet, through their own devices, their basic biological needs and other necessary conditions for human agency.

In light of this sort of argument, it might be time for America to reconsider its traditional doctrine that an employer can fire whomever he wants "at will", that is, without cause, but in any case, the country has moved to exempt from the general "at will" doctrine groups against whom discrimination is widespread enough that it short-circuits the general features of competition that tend to place people in the jobs for which they are best suited.

If gays were barred only from buying rocks at Tiffany's, eating truffles at 21, and holding seats on the Board of Trade, their inclusion in civil rights laws on the ground that such laws help meet needs would not be very compelling. And indeed America holds a stereotype of gays, especially gay men, as wealthy, frivolous, selfish, conspicuous consumers. In 1996, Justice Scalia in his dissent to *Romer v. Evans*—discussed below—claimed that "those who engage in homosexual conduct tend to reside in disproportionate numbers in certain communities, have high disposable income, and of course care about homosexual-rights issues much more ardently than the public at large."[2] Based on this stereotype of gays as wealthy, power-hungry, self-centered snobs, some people claim that gays are not in need of civil rights protections. But the stereotype is false. One of the surprising findings of Alfred Kinsey's 1948 study of male sexuality was that more male homosexual behavior occurs among the economically disadvantaged and among the uneducated than among the wealthy and college educated. And it is generally acknowledged that lesbians on average fall well below the national average for income, if for no other reason than that women are so far below the national average for income.[3]

One of the little-sung heroes of the gay movement is John F. Singer. On June 26, 1972, Singer was fired from the Equal Employment Opportunity Commission. He was fired for being gay. His case took six years in front of numerous courts and administrative panels before he was vindicated. Along the way, it helped force the federal government to change its administrative policies toward lesbians and gays in civil service jobs. When fired, he held the position of filing clerk.

Extending civil rights protection to gay men and lesbians is also justified as promoting general prosperity. Such legislation tends to increase the production of goods and services for society as a whole. It does so in three ways.

First, by eliminating extraneous factors in employment decisions, such legislation promotes an optimal fit between a worker's capacities and the tasks of his prospective work. Both the worker and her employer are advantaged, because a worker is most productive when her talents and the requirements of her job mesh. Across the business community as a whole, such legislation further enhances the prospects that talent does not go wasting and that job vacancies are not filled by second bests.

In response to prospective discrimination, gay men and lesbians are prone to take jobs that only partially use their talents or that squander them on trivial pursuits. Many lesbians and gay men take dead-end jobs, which do not use their full capacities; they do so in order to avoid reviews that might reveal their minority status and result in their dismissal. Many gay men and lesbians go into small business because too frequently big business will not have them. In turn, many small businesses or dead-end occupations, like being a florist, hairdresser, male nurse, or female trucker or construction worker, have in society's mind become so closely associated with homosexuality that nongays who might otherwise go into these lines of employment do not do so out of fear that they will be socially branded as deviant. In these circumstances, the talents of people—both gay and nongay—are simply wasted both to themselves and to society. Rights for gay folk are good for everyone.

Second, human resources are wasted if one's energies are constantly diverted and devoured by fear of arbitrary dismissal. The cost of life in the closet is not small, for the closet permeates and largely consumes the life of its occupant. In the absence of civil rights legislation for lesbians and gay men, society is wasting the human resources that are expended in the day-to-day anxiety—the web of lies, the constant worry—that attends leading a life of systematic disguise as a condition for continued employment.

Third, employment makes up a large part of what happiness is. To a large extent, happiness is job satisfaction. When a person's employment is of a favorable sort, he or she finds a delight in its very execution—quite independent of any object that the job generates, whether product or wage. People whose work on its own is rich enough and interesting enough to count as a personal flourishing, people, for instance, employed in human services, academics, and other professionals, and people whose job entails a large element of craft, like editors and artisans, are indeed likely to view job satisfaction as a major constituent of happiness and rank it high both qualitatively and quantitatively among the sources of happiness. And even people who are forced by necessity or misfortune to take up employment that does not use their talents, or that is virtually mechanical, or positively dangerous, or that has other conditions that make the workplace hateful—even these people are likely to recognize that the workplace, if properly arranged, would be a locus of happiness, and this recognition of opportunity missed is part of the frustration that accompanies jobs that are necessarily unsatisfying to perform. To permit discriminatory hiring practices is to reduce happiness generally by impeding access to one of its main sources.

Civil rights legislation also promotes individual flourishing—not merely by enhancing the prospect that individuals' needs are met, but more so by expanding the ranges of individual choice. Government has a perceived obligation to enhance conditions that promote the flourishing of individual modes of living. Thus for example, the general rationale for compulsory liberal education is that such compulsion ultimately issues in autonomous individuals capable of making decisions for themselves from a field of alternative opinions. Analogously, civil rights legislation, though a somewhat coercive force in the marketplace, promotes those conditions that enable people to draw up and carry out life plans of their own making.

Such legislation withdraws the threat of punishment by social banishment, loss of employment, and the like from the arsenal of majoritarian coercion, so that individual lives need not be molded by social conventions and by the demands of conformity set by others. The result of such legislation is that the means by which one lives shall not be permitted to serve as instruments for the despotism of custom.

This justification for civil rights legislation also has special import for gay men and lesbians. With the lessening of fear from threat of discovery, ordinary gays will begin to lead self-determining lives. Imagine the lives of those gay men and lesbians who systematically forgo the opportunity of sharing the common necessities of life and of sharing the emotional dimensions of intimacy as the price for the means by which they place bread on their table. Love and caring could cost you your job—if you're gay—while catch-as-catch-can sex and intimacy could cost you your life.

In the absence of civil rights legislation, lesbians and gay men are placed in the position of having to make zero-sum trade-offs between the components that go into making a full life, trade-offs, say, between a reasonable personal life and employment, trade-offs that the majority would not tolerate for themselves even for a minute.

\* \* \*

As an invisible minority, gay men and lesbians also need civil rights protections in order for them to have reasonably guaranteed access to an array of fundamental rights that virtually everyone would agree are supposed to pertain equally to all people.

By "invisible minority," I mean a minority whose members can be identified only through an act of will on someone's part, rather than merely through observation of the members' day-to-day actions in the public domain. Thus severely physically and mentally challenged people would rank along with racial classes, gender classes, and some ethnic and religious groups (like the Amish) as visible minorities, whereas diabetics, assimilated Jews, Lutherans, atheists, and released prisoners would rank along with gay men and lesbians as invisible minorities.

For the sake of argument, let us presume the acceptability of a governmental system that is a constitutionally regulated representative democracy with a developed body of civic law. Such in broad outline is the government of the United States and its various states. Then, civil rights for gay men and lesbians are a necessary precondition for the proper functioning of this system.

First, civil rights legislation for gay men and lesbians is warranted as being necessary for gays having equitable access to civic rights. By "civic rights," I mean rights to the impartial administration of civil and criminal law in defense of property and person. In the absence of such rights, there is no rule of law. An invisible minority historically subjected to widespread social discrimination has reasonably guaranteed access to these rights only when the minority is guaranteed nondiscrimination in employment, housing, and public services.

All would agree that civic rights are rights that everyone is supposed to have. All individuals must be assured the right to demand from government access to judicial procedures. But imagine the following scenario. Steve, who teaches math at a private suburban high school and coaches the swim team, on a weekend night heads to a popular gay bar. There he meets Tom, a self-employed contractor and father of two boys whose mother does not want Tom to have visitation rights, but is ignorant of his new life. Tom and Steve decide to walk to Tom's nearby flat, which he rents from a bigot who bemoans the fact that the community is going gay and refuses to rent to people he supposes to be gay. Tom's weekend visitations from his sons are his cover.

Meanwhile, at a nearby youth home for orphaned teenagers, the leader of one gang is taunting Tony, the leader of another gang, with the accusation of being a faggot. After much protestation, Tony claims he will prove once and for all that he is not a faggot, and hits the streets with his gang members, who tote with them the blunt and not-so-blunt instruments of the queerbasher's trade. Like a hyena pack upon a wildebeest, they descend on Tom and Steve, downing their victims in a blizzard of strokes and blows. Local residents coming home from parties and others walking their dogs witness the whole event.

Imagine that two miracles occur. One, a squad car happens by, and two, the police actually do their job. Tony and another of the fleeing queerbashers are caught and arrested on the felony charges of aggravated assault and attempted murder. Other squad cars arrive, and while witnesses' reports are gathered, Steve and Tom are taken to the nearest emergency room. Once Steve and Tom are in wards, the police arrive to take statements of complaint from them in what appears to be an open-and-shut case. But Steve knows the exposure of his sexual orientation in a trial will terminate his employment. And Tom knows the exposure of a trial would give his ex-wife the legal excuse she desires to deny his visitation rights. And he knows he will eventually lose his apartment. So neither man can reasonably risk pressing charges. They de facto become hostile witnesses to their own cause. Tony is released, and within twelve hours of attempting murder, he returns to the youth home hailed by all as a conquering hero. Rights for gays are a necessary condition for judicial access.

Any reader of gay urban tabloids knows that the events sketched here—miracles excepted—occur all too frequently. Many lesbians and gay men are in effect blackmailed by our judicial system. Our judicial system's threat of exposure prevents gay access to judicial protections. The example given above of latter-day lynch law falls within the sphere of criminal justice. Even more obviously, the same judicial blackmail occurs in civil cases.

It is unreasonable to expect anyone to give up that by which she lives, her employment, her shelter, her access to goods and services and to loved ones in order for judicial procedures to be carried out equitably, in order to demand legal protections.

Now what is paradoxical about this blackmail by the judiciary is that in the absence of civil rights legislation, the blackmail is a necessary consequence of two major virtues of the fair administration of justice with its determinations of guilt and innocence being based on a full examination of the facts. The first virtue is that trials are open to scrutiny by public and press. The second is that defendants must be able to be confronted by the witnesses against them and have compulsory process for obtaining witnesses in their favor, while conversely prosecutors must have the tools with which to press cases on behalf of victims. The result of these two virtues is that trials cast the private into the public realm.

That trials cast the private into the public realm puts the lie to those who claim that what gays do in private is no one else's business and should not be anyone else's business, so that on the one hand, gays do not need rights and on the other hand, they do not deserve rights, lest they make themselves public. If the judiciary system is to be open and fair, it is necessary that gays be granted civil rights. Otherwise judicial access becomes a right only for the dominant culture.

Widespread social prejudice against lesbians and gay men also has the effect of eclipsing their political rights. In the absence of gay civil rights legislation, gays are—over the range of issues that most centrally affect their minority status—effectively denied access to the political rights of the First Amendment, that is, freedom of speech, freedom of press, freedom of assembly, and freedom to petition for the redress of grievances. In addition, they are especially denied the emergent constitutional right of association—an amalgam of the freedoms of speech and assembly—which establishes the right to join and be identified with other persons for common political goals.

Put concretely, does a gay person who has to laugh at and manufacture fag jokes in the workplace in order to deflect suspicion in an office that routinely fires gay employees have freedom to express his or her views on gay issues? Is it likely that such a person could reasonably risk appearing in public at a gay rights rally? Would such a person be able to participate in a march celebrating the Stonewall Riots and the start of gay activism? Would such a person be able to sign, let alone circulate, a petition protesting the firing of a gay worker? Would such a person likely try to persuade workmates to vote for a gay-positive city councilman? Would such a person sign a letter to the editor protesting abusive reportage of gay issues and events, or advocating the discussion of gay issues in schools? The answer to all these questions is "obviously not." Such a person is usually so transfixed by fear that it is highly unlikely that he or she could even be persuaded to write out a check to a gay rights organization.

Further, as a group that is a permanent (statistical) minority, it is hardly fair for gays to be additionally encumbered in politics by having a plurality of its members absent through social coercion from the public workings of the political process.

If First Amendment rights are not to be demoted to privileges to which only the dominant culture has access, then invisible minorities that are subject to widespread social discrimination will have to be guaranteed protection from those forces that maintain them in their position of invisibility. Civil rights protections take a very long step in that direction.

For at a minimum, all potentially effective political activity requires widely and pointedly disseminated political ideas. Only then is it possible for a minority political position on social policy to have a chance of becoming the majority opinion and so of becoming government policy and law. If the majority of people never have the occasion to change their opinions to those of a minority position, political rights would be pointless. Not surprisingly, then, public actions predominate among the actions protected by the First Amendment—speaking, publishing, petitioning, assembling, associating.

Now, a person who is a member of an invisible minority and who must remain invisible, hidden, and secreted in respect to her minority status as a condition for maintaining a livelihood is not free to be public about her minority status or to incur suspicion by publicly associating with others who are open about their similar status. And so she is effectively denied all political power—except the right to vote. But voting aside, she will be denied the freedom to express her views in a public forum and to unite with or organize other like-minded individuals in an attempt to compete for votes that would elect persons who will support the policies advocated by her group. She is denied all effective use of legally available means of influencing public opinion prior to voting and all effective means of lobbying after elections are held.

To get a sense of how poorly gay men and lesbians are positioned to represent their interests in legislative and executive forums, consider that the national lesbian and gay Political Action Committee, the Victory Fund, reports in 2004 that of the half a million elected government officials in America only 275 are openly gay or lesbian. Thirteen states have no out gay men or lesbians in any elected office. Twenty-six state legislatures are without any openly lesbian or gay members.[4] Though gay men and lesbians are now well represented by the fourth estate, they are barely a trace in the third.

It would seem incumbent upon government, then, to work toward ending those social conditions and mechanisms by which majority opinion maintains itself simply by the elimination of the hearing of possible alternative policies. To this end, government must prohibit nongovernmental agents from interfering with the political activities of individuals and groups. Thus, for instance, not only are political rallies constitutionally immune from government interference but also government is positively obliged to prohibit goon squads and hecklers from disrupting political rallies. Analogously, bigoted employers, landlords, and the like are the subtle goon squads and hecklers who deny gay men and lesbians access to political rights.

Up to the AIDS crisis, the meager energies and monies of the gay rights movement were directed almost exclusively at trying to secure civil rights protections for lesbians and gay men. Without these legislated rights, which begin to bring gays into the procedures of democracy, gays have not been able to act very effectively on the issues about which gays reasonably would want to exert influence in democratic policy-making. By being hobbled in the public procedures of democracy, gays are inadequately positioned to defend their own interests on substantial issues of vital concern.

It was thinking along these general lines that led to the only post-Stonewall gay win before the Supreme Court other than 2003's *Lawrence v. Texas* sodomy decision. In 1996, the Court in *Romer v. Evans* ruled that Colorado could not add an amendment to its state constitution picking out gays as the one and only group for which the state legislature was barred from passing civil rights protections.[5] This case, also written by Justice Kennedy, is, like his *Lawrence* opinion, hardly a model of clear thought and expression, but he seemed, at least in part, to reason that states cannot selectively cast up barriers to participation in the processes of government. Democracy must be "open on impartial terms to all who seek [the government's] assistance. A state cannot deem a class of persons a stranger to its laws."

\* \* \*

These various arguments should have a compelling cumulative force in justifying civil rights laws and the inclusion of lesbians and gay men within their protected classes. Still, some people argue that there are legitimate reasons for exempting lesbians and gay men from some specific applications of general civil rights protections. Indeed the 1964 Civil Rights Act itself reasonably enough allows exemptions for discrimination against an otherwise protected category when the discrimination represents a "bona fide occupational qualification" reasonably necessary to the normal operation of a particular business or enterprise. For example, church-related hiring decisions may be made on religiously based distinctions. Are there some discriminations against gays that constitute such morally allowable "good faith" distinction-drawing? Not as a general matter.

Though the parameters of good faith discrimination are somewhat murky, the following general principle governing the establishment of such discriminations can be gleaned from our culture's moral experience. The principle is that simply citing the current existence of prejudice, bigotry, or discrimination in a society against some group or citing the obvious consequences of such prejudice, bigotry, or discrimination can never constitute a good reason in trying to establish a good faith discrimination against that group. The principle means that stigmas that are socially induced may not play a part in rational moral deliberations, that rationales for discrimination cannot be bootstrapped off of amassed private biases. For instance, a community could not legitimately claim that a bylaw banning blacks from buying houses in the community was a good faith discrimination on the ground that whenever blacks move into a previously all-white area, property values plummet. This rationale is illegitimate, since current bigotry and its consequences are the only causes of the property values dropping—the result of white flight and the subsequent reduction in the size of the purchasing market.

In general, the fact that people discriminate can never be cited as a good reason for institutionalizing discrimination. But even more clearly, the current existence of discrimination cannot ethically ground the continuance of the discrimination in the face of a moral presumption against discrimination. To hold otherwise is to admit the validity of the heckler's veto: to hold that it is acceptable for the state to prevent a speaker from speaking when a heckler in advance threatens disruption if the speaker does speak.

The reach of the principle is broad, because its obvious ranges of application include cases where some joint project is a necessary part of a job. It is in this category of cases that good faith discriminations against gays are most often attempted.

Bans against gays in the armed forces and on police forces provide classic cases of attempts to establish good faith discrimination. In the early 1980s, the Pentagon articulated six reasons for banning gays from the armed forces: "The presence of such members adversely affects the ability of the armed forces [1] to maintain discipline, good order and morale, [2] to foster mutual trust and confidence among servicemembers, [3] to insure the integrity of the system of rank and command, [4] to facilitate assignment and worldwide deployment of servicemembers who frequently must live and work under close conditions affording minimal privacy, [5] to recruit and retain members of the armed forces, [and 6] to maintain the public acceptability of military service."[6]

What all these claims have negatively in common is that none of them is based on the ability of gay and lesbian soldiers to fulfill the duties of their stations. More generally, none of the claims is based on gays *doing* anything at all. What the six reasons have positively in common is that their force relies exclusively on current widespread bigoted attitudes against lesbians and gay men. They appeal to the bigotry and consequent disruptiveness of nongay soldiers (reasons 1, 2, 3, 4, and 5), who apparently are made "up-tight" by the mere presence of gay soldiers and officers, and so claim that they cannot work effectively in necessary joint projects with gay soldiers. The reasons appeal to the antigay prejudices of our own society (reason 6), especially that segment of it that constitutes potential recruits (reason 5), and to the antigay prejudices of other societies (reason 4). No reasons other than currently existing widespread prejudice and bigotry of others are appealed to here in order to justify a discriminatory policy against lesbians and gay men. So all six reasons violate the principle of good faith. Indeed the military's rationales are eerily reminiscent of the military's rationales for segregating troops by race until President Truman ended the policy by executive order in 1948.

Another argument in which bad faith parades as good faith is one that tries to justify discrimination against gay teachers. It runs as follows: though openly gay teachers do not cause their students to become gay, an openly gay teacher might (inadvertently or not) cause a closeted gay student to become openly gay; the life of an openly gay person is a life of misery and suffering; therefore, openly gay teachers must be fired, since they promote misery and suffering. It seems that the second premise—life of misery—if true in some way peculiar to gays, is so in the main as the result of currently existing bigotry and discrimination in society of the very sort that the argument tries to enshrine into school board policy. So this argument too violates the principle of good faith.

The three-judge dissent from the Massachusetts supreme court's 2004 ruling that civil unions would not pass constitutional muster as a substitute for gay marriages relied entirely on appeals to ongoing prejudice and discrimination against gays to try to justify the restriction of the term "marriage" to heterosexuals—discrimination against gays by the federal government in the Defense of Marriage Act, by states that have passed their own mini-DOMAs, and by society in general, which the dissenting judges pointed out would continue to take gays' relationships less seriously than straights' even if lesbian and gay couples were allowed the use of the term "marriage." Such discrimination, the dissenters argued, disposed gays differently than straights in relation to the term "marriage," and so warranted a different legal language to be used of gay relationships. To all this, the four-judge opinion of the court correctly answered: "That such prejudice exists is not a reason to insist on less than the Constitution requires."[7]

Take as a final example of accumulated prejudice parading as good faith discrimination the arguments typically used in lesbian child custody cases. As of 2000, four states—Alabama, Mississippi, Missouri, and Virginia—continued to apply categorical presumptions against lesbian and gay parents in custody cases. Elsewhere, despite the near universal adoption of the gender-neutral "best interest of the child" test for determining which parent gets custody of a child, actual legal practice in nearly all jurisdictions still operates on a strong presumption in favor of giving custody to the mother *unless* the mother is a lesbian, in which case the presumption of parental fitness shifts sharply in the direction of the father. In 1996, a Florida appeals court in Tallahassee awarded custody of a lesbian's twelve-year-old daughter to the girl's father, even though he had served eight years in prison for murdering his first wife.[8] Sometimes the argument for this sharp shift is merely a statement of bigotry and stereotype. It runs: lesbians are immoral; lesbians cause their children to become lesbians; and therefore, lesbians cause their children to be immoral. When the shift is attempted to be justified as a good faith discrimination, the argument runs as follows: there is nothing inherently evil about mother or child being lesbian, but nevertheless, since, while the child is growing, there will be strong social recrimination from peers and other parents against the child as it becomes known in the community that the mother is a lesbian, only by discriminating against lesbian mothers are their children spared unnecessary suffering. In 1995, the Virginia supreme court using such reasoning went so far as to give custody of a lesbian's son to a third party, her mother, claiming that "living daily under conditions stemming from active lesbianism practiced in the home may impose a burden upon a child by reason of the 'social condemnation' attached to such an arrangement, which will inevitably afflict the child's relationships with its peers and with the community."[9] In January 2004, a Tennessee appeals court removed custody rights from a recently out father, claiming, "The father's homosexuality may not influence his parenting ability per se. However, the father's decision to openly co-habit with his partner is a change that will generate questions from his daughters and their friends regarding their father's lifestyle."[10] Here again bad faith is masquerading as good. In these cases, current bigotry and its consequences are cited as the only reason for perpetrating and institutionalizing discrimination. No one would seriously suggest that a fat mother or a Mormon mother should lose custody of her child because the child's friends might well tease the child about her mother's size or religion. Clearly the "argument" is a mask of prejudice.

In 1984, the Supreme Court in *Palmore v. Sidoti* unanimously rejected the claim that recriminations that come to a child because her mother marries someone of another race can be legitimately taken into account in custody cases. The Court held, "The question ... is whether the reality of private biases and the possible injury they might inflict are permissible considerations [in justifying discrimination]. We have little difficulty concluding that they are not. The Constitution cannot control ... prejudices but neither can it tolerate them. Private biases may be outside the reach of the law, but the law cannot, directly or indirectly, give them effect."[11] If this general principle were applied consistently in gay and lesbian cases, the end of official discrimination against gay people would be in sight.

## Chapter 6

# Understanding Lesbians and Gay Men in the Military

From the Second World War through the first Gulf War, the United States military excluded from service anyone it considered to be homosexual. Then, in 1993, the country adopted a more complicated policy. By federal statute, the military is barred from asking its members whether they are gay, but is required to discharge any member who says he or she is gay.[1] The policy is popularly dubbed "don't ask, don't tell." On average, a thousand lesbian and gay soldiers have been dismissed each year under the policy from 1993 to 2003.[2] The policy is not one which can be morally acceptable to gay men and lesbians, or indeed to anyone who has respect for human beings.

The past policy of rooting out and totally excluding gay men and lesbians at least had the virtue of treating gays as devils—evil forces set on destruction and corruption. As we know from Dante and Milton, devils can be charming, vibrant, intriguing fellows. Devils are even creatures worthy of respect for who they are, though not for what they do. After all, they are at heart angels—angels who have gone wrong and do wrong. And devils, remember, are creatures about whom we can talk, indeed should talk, so we can find them out.

The moral dynamics of "don't ask, don't tell" treat lesbians and gay men differently and worse. In this policy, gay men and lesbians are not demonized as agents to be feared for what they might do, but rather are viewed as the horrible, the disgusting, the loathsome, the unspeakably gross—in short, as abject beings. Core cases of the abject are excrement, vomit, pus, and the smells associated with these. Such repulsive matters are expelled from the body's insides in its very process of living, but tend to cling to it, and so are always in need of being cleansed away.

It is just exactly around these (only ever half-acknowledged) abject matters that society sets up rituals of the form "don't ask, don't tell." Take, for example, the case of flatulence in a crowded elevator: no one tells; no one asks; everyone acts as though nothing is amiss, and so reinforces the abject thing's status as loathsome. When faced or confronted with the abject, people have visceral responses of aversion, distraction, vertigo, even nausea, and so, to the extent possible, people systematically act like the abject does not exist, even though they secretly and deeply know it does.

This daunting effort to repress knowing and acknowledgment requires a blanket of silence to be cast over the abject thing. In order to be systematic, the silence must be ritualized: to tell of the abject is to break a taboo; for names, like scents, bring abject matters back fully to consciousness. And, to ask of the abject is to be reminded of its constantly recurring, lurking, louring presence just beyond oneself.

In essence, the Pentagon order "don't ask, don't tell" ritualizes into a national paradigm The Closet—with its open secret and commitment to the abject standing and worthlessness of lesbian and gay people. The order says that as long as *you* gays act as though *we* people don't know who you are, we will act as though you don't exist, and thus in our willing ignorance, recommit ourselves to viewing your status as loathsome and repulsive.

The chief problem of the social institution of the closet is not that it promotes hypocrisy, requires lies, sets snares, blames the victim when snared, and causes unhappiness—though it does have all these results. No, the chief problem with the closet is that it treats gays as less than human, less than animal, less even than vegetable—it treats gays as reeking scum, the breath of death. No one can accept the "don't ask, don't tell" policy and suppose that at the same time he or she is treating lesbians and gay men as persons.

Polls have detected in the general population a major shift afoot toward a willingness to accept lesbians and gay men in the military. A CNN/USA Today/Gallup poll conducted in early December 2003 found that 79 percent of Americans overall were supportive of allowing gays to serve openly; 91 percent of people aged eighteen to twenty-nine were supportive, as were 85 percent of all women, 73 percent of all men, and 74 percent of southerners.[3] I argue that the nation as a whole will be the chief gainer if the policy is changed.

The gain I imagine, though, is not primarily the pragmatic one that the armed forces would operate better as an armed force. Still it is noteworthy in this regard that over the last ten years Canada, Israel, and Britain have dropped their bans on gays serving openly in their armies—without incident.[4] And consider: after the September 11, 2001, terrorist attacks on the Pentagon and World Trade Center, the U.S. military was frantic to recruit speakers of Arabic. But between October 2001 and September 2002, the army went on to discharge for being gay six of its Arabic language specialists from the Defense Language Institute in Monterey, California, the military's primary language training school.[5] Prudence alone suggests dropping the policy.

But the chief benefit of change would take place on the plane of the nation's ideals. In dropping the ban, the nation would adopt an improved understanding of what citizenship is. Despite the recent polls, getting Congress to drop the ban will be a daunting task just exactly because of the role the military plays in the nation's thinking about itself and, in turn, the role the gay ban plays in the military's thinking about itself. Indeed the ban on gays in the military goes to the heart of the nation's and the military's gut feelings about what it means to be a person. The ban, therefore, can be adequately understood only in cultural terms.

The military is nominally intended to *defend* what the country is, but as its racial and gender histories show, it is one of the chief institutions by which the nation *defines* what the country is and what is to count as full personhood and full citizenship. Take the Civil War. Even though the North was fighting (at least in part) to end black slavery, both North and South initially conceived the war as one to be carried out only between white men—full citizens. President Lincoln (it may come as a surprise to learn) was not seeking full citizenship for blacks, did not entertain black equal protection, and opposed the black vote. He thought blacks should be like white women as far as citizenship was concerned. But under the press of necessity, both sides, by war's end, had resorted to the deployment of black combat troops. For many southerners, this reconfiguration of the army was the equivalent of having lost the war even before hostilities were over. For in being combatants, blacks had changed their definition and assumed the rank of full citizens. They could no longer be thought of as slaves. The North cast this conceptual shift into institutional, indeed constitutional form. The Fourteenth Amendment granted full citizenship and equal protection rights to blacks, and the Fifteenth Amendment conferred the vote on black men. At least on the plane of the nation's *ideals*, the Civil War and its amendments catapulted the nation far ahead of Lincoln's understanding of race.

The ban on homosexual presence in the military operates at a similar profound level of national definition. Straight male soldiers' skittishness, which the military uses to try to justify the suppression of any gay male presence in the armed forces, is a mere surface phenomenon masking a much deeper and wider cultural anxiety about gay men—anxiety over understanding the male body as a penetrable object. For the military, the real person, the full citizen, is defined as one who must penetrate while never being penetrated. Conversely, it defines the enemy as a potentially penetrating but actually penetrated body. The citizen warrior first "penetrates" the enemy's lines and then penetrates the enemy himself for the kill.

But with the development of military tactics and technologies in the opening decades of the twentieth century, notions of what is penetrated and what counts as penetration became fuzzy in practice. Battle lines became vague. And those sturdy penetrators—sword, lance, and bayonet—gave way to strafing, remote bombing, gas, and radiation as what kills. War became foggier than ever. The resulting ambiguity in military practice called for a refocusing and resolidification of the distinction between the penetrable and the impenetrable at the level of the military's conception of itself. And so with the coming of the Second World War, general exclusions from the military for immorality crystallized in 1942 into an explicit ban on homosexual soldiers.

The categories of male heterosexual and male homosexual definition provide both the cultural symbols for and social undergirding to our contemporary understanding of battle and citizenship. To allow gay men—willingly penetrable penetrators—to go into battle would be (so it goes) to confuse warriors with the enemy, full citizens with those worthy of death, to confuse conquest and defeat, glory and damnation.

Gen. Norman Schwartzkopf stated as much when in 1993, as the celebrated leader of the American forces during the first Gulf War, he testified before Congress against lifting the ban on gays—he was thinking of gay men—in the military. He told Congress that to have gay men serving openly in the military would cause U.S. combat troops to wilt as Iraqi troops did in 1991 when they passively "sat in the desserts of Kuwait forced to execute orders they did not believe in," lay down their weapons, and waited for his U.S. forces to sweep over them.[6] Capitol watchers pointed to this testimony as the death knell for attempts to lift the ban.

My analysis also explains—and is bolstered by—the traditional defining of women out of combat roles, roles that call for shooting guns at and stabbing the enemy. In the modern army, it is socially acceptable for women to be killed in battle—while, for instance, laying communication wires across the battle front or flying troop transport planes through battle zones. So, paternalistic arguments tendered to explain the barring of women from combat roles—"it's for their own good"—simply do not track military reality. Rather if women—culturally viewed essentially as penetrable bodies—were to be killers, combatants, and so conceptualized not as penetrable bodies but as penetrators, that again would challenge the definition of full citizens as impenetrable bodies and the enemy as penetrable bodies. The real reason, the deep reason, why women have traditionally been barred from combat and gay people (culturally read, gay men) have traditionally been barred from the military altogether is that the exclusions are essential machinery in the cultural project that defines full citizens as impenetrable penetrators.

This analysis may seem to collide with statistics that strongly suggest lesbians are discharged from the military at a disproportionately higher rate than gay men.[7] The explanation of this phenomenon, I suggest, is that lesbians or rather lesbianism, the idea, is serving as a substitute for women in general. Charges of lesbianism provide convenient excuses for the military mind to carry out an ideology that says women simply do not belong in the armed forces, that the nature of woman is incompatible with that which makes real men real men. Remember the tremendous resistance to genderal integration at American military academies.[8] So charges of lesbianism and the selective efforts, witch hunts, if you will, to track down lesbians are somewhat similar to the Nazis' use of the charge of homosexuality to root out Catholic clergy, whom in general they did not like.[9] Social pressures prevented the Nazis from directly attacking priests as Catholic, as ersatz Jehovah's Witnesses. Catholic Bavaria, after all, was the Nazis' home base. And so the Nazis laid charges of perversion against unwanted priests. It worked. Civilian social pressures prevent the military mind from directly attacking women as women, so it uses as a substitute charges of homosexuality. It's working.

My analysis also explains how the military operates in extremis. Consider how the U.S. army now ritualizes soldiers' bodies when it commemorates the fallen, the penetrated. It tries to resolidify the vision of the soldier as impenetrable penetrator. At memorials, the fallen soldier is represented by his boots, bayoneted rifle, and helmet. The rifle's bayonet is stabbed into Mother Earth slightly behind the boots, while its butt is crowned with the soldier's helmet. The bayoneted—bayoneting—rifle—all blade and steel—is the stand-in for, the symbol of, the soldier's body, which, in turn and ritual, emblemizes his soul, his true nature.[10] No weak, pierceable flesh here. By contrast, fifth-century Attic Greece commemorated its fallen by carving full-body profiles of soldiers on outsize marble tombstones. A soldier is depicted in midstride holding a spear in his outward hand, a shield with his inward. He wears sandals and a helmet, but nothing else.[11] The fragile, radiant beauty of his fully articulated, completely naked body images the soul.

Lifting the ban on gay soldiers will not only, finally, acknowledge the full status of gays as citizens in America—important as that recognition is on its own—but also begin, as did the ending of slavery, to transform our understanding of who we are as people. It will change our ideals, whatever our failed or partial practices of them may be. The ending of slavery meant that a person may no longer view another essentially as just an instrument or tool in his or her own projects. The end of the military's ban on gay male presence will extend this line of cultural thinking and point in the direction of equally momentous cultural change and moral improvement.

It will allow everyone to have a more relaxed view of human agency and to experience the universe as a more hospitable, commodious and, in turn, respect-worthy abode. The citizen need not define himself as conqueror, need not view the universe and others as something that must be subjugated to or killed by his intrusive presence in order to be good. One need not invade others to be what one is. One may be open to being, rather than stand in opposition to it. Reason can then include a healthy element of contemplation, rather than remaining limited to instrumental uses, calculations of utility, and the analysis of things into manageable parts. We will be less in need of grace, for we shall be more graceful. We will be less in need of divine intervention, for we will stand more receptive to each other. We can worry less about being ineffectual and weak. We will be more merciful to those who fail, for we will have less to prove in ourselves. A kinder, gentler nation will finally become a live possibility. We will be more self-contained and self-confident, even as we are more easily able to make connections with each other. We will be more productive when we view productivity as creation and care rather than as management and control. We will be more self-sufficient, as we release for individual flourishing the massive cultural energy now wasted in the anxiety required to prop up the false symbol of self-sufficiency—impenetrability.

Straight male soldiers who are unable to follow along with society on this journey of transformation can always stoop rather than bend over for soap dropped in the shower.

## Conclusion

## America's Promise and
## the Lesbian and Gay Future

A perplexity: at the dawn of the twenty-first century, just as lesbians and gay men were making slow, steady, incremental progress in the direction of social and legal equality, interest in lesbian and gay issues suddenly exploded across the national scene and gay folk themselves significantly raised the bar up the standards of what they wanted, expected, and were willing to fight for. Chief among the new expectations was access to full marriage rights, something that gay organizations, both state and national, had not before pegged as a high priority. Indeed, when it came to same-sex marriage, gay political organizations had been saying to their constituents, "Go slow; be cautious; above all else, do no harm." Strangely, incremental progress did not dissipate reformist energies or produce satisfaction in what gays had already achieved. Just the opposite happened.

What is driving America's violet velvet revolution? Two things. First, gay men and lesbians rethinking what is possible. Second, gay men and lesbians rethinking what it means to be gay and lesbian.

The first impulse, as gay columnist Paul Varnell has pointed out, is an example of what Alexis de Tocqueville dubbed "the revolution of rising expectations." De Tocqueville observed that the French Revolution did not occur when the masses were crushed and desperate, oppressed and without resources, rather the revolution occurred when prosperity was on the rise and intimations of liberty were in the air. He put it this way:

> It is not always in going from bad to worse that one falls into revolution. It more often happens that a people who have borne without complaint, as if they did not feel them, the most burdensome laws, reject them violently once their weight is lightened ... . The inevitable evil that one bears patiently seems unbearable as soon as one conceives the idea of removing it. Every abuse that is then eliminated seems to highlight those that remain and makes them feel more biting; the evil has decreased, it is true, but the sensitivity to it is greater.[1]

This revolution of rising expectations fits recent gay and lesbian experience nicely. When gay men and lesbians began to conceive of the elements of marriage coming to them piecemeal and partial through domestic partnership registries, corporate largesse, and the like, they suddenly recognized what they still did not have and how unjust that lack is. A similar revolution swept gays' allies. When justice began to seem a live possibility, they were prompted by its call, even, in the case of some brave mayors and clergy, to the point of performing acts of civil disobedience in order to officiate at gay and lesbian civil weddings.[2] When, in this way, citizens are motivated by goodness rather than (just) self-interest, America is likely to see not only a rise in pressure on politicians to do *some thing*, but also a rise in national consciousness to do the *right thing*.

The second source of the sudden press for justice configured around same-sex marriage is a rising level of consciousness among lesbians and gay men themselves—in particular, a dawning recognition that gayness is a form of connectedness. Too often, gays and our allies have argued that gayness does not matter, that gayness is irrelevant—that, after all, gays are "just people too." These rhetorical moves are inadvertent, even well intentioned, erasures of gayness. They suppose that gayness is a property, like having an eye color or wearing an earring, that a person could have in isolation from all other people and without significant effect on others. And it is perfectly understandable that gays and others have in the past taken up this stance as a major premise in arguments and calls for lesbian and gay rights.

First, the lesbian and gay rights movement, for the longest part of its duration, was singularly focused on civil rights legislation. Indeed, in the 1970s and early 1980s, if one used the expression "gay rights," one was presumed to be speaking of legislated civil rights for gays. And in this context, if gayness is irrelevant in general, then presumptively it is irrelevant to flying a plane, serving a meal, teaching a class, or being a cop. And so it would be unjust for society to discriminate on the basis of sexual orientation, since sexual orientation is not the basis for anything—or so it goes.

Second, if gayness is an irrelevant property, then it is easier to make analogies between gayness and race, especially if (as per one of the Right's main fantasies) race is viewed simply as a matter of skin color and not as a system of cultural expectations and subcultural inventions. Finally, the view that gayness doesn't matter had a strategic pull. If a person's being gay were an irrelevant characteristic, then other people would not have to be so afraid of it, afraid that they might be it or get it. As a tactic against persecution and a plea for tolerance, it wasn't a bad strategy. But if lesbians and gay men stick with this view, we will be stuck indeed.

In our social projects, gay men and lesbians need to be thinking more of gayness not as something that a person can have in splendid isolation from others. It takes two to be queer.

We need to conceptualize gayness as a relational property, a human bonding, one in need of tendance and social concern. Gayness places or situates the gay person in social and interpersonal contexts. It is both an outflow and a reception of perception, desire, affection, and knowing—both biblical and cognitive. We need to stop claiming that gayness is an irrelevant property and begin recognizing that it is crucially important to people's lives and identities, to social history, and, as the "queer theory" crowd is showing, to understanding central components of many of society's most important concepts and cherished institutions.[3]

The reason that gay marriage has become such a major issue for gays is that both gayness and marriage have their roots in everyday existence. Marriage becomes a way of incorporating gayness as connectedness into the everyday. It should not be surprising then that gay men and lesbians—as a matter of pride and need—are shifting issues of family life to the top of our political agenda. Gay sex, gay love, gay life, and gay presence all matter.

*  *  *

Whether American law at large allows gays and marriage to merge or permanently blocks their union will depend on whether the cultural, social, and private sector progress now under way on gay issues induces a force field in the minds of the makers and interpreters of law sufficient to affect their deliberations. Such progress on substantive issues has been impressive, even if still partial and contested, especially around the issue of gayness as connection.

*Take religion.* Catholicism, at least the Catholic hierarchy, has dug in its heels on gay issues. The reason: if in society's eye, gayness turns out to be acceptable, then the church loses the last clear example, and so too the intuitive appeal, of its view that morality is somehow grounded in the structures of nature—that good actions are those that follow nature, bad those that are unnatural, run "contrary to nature." With the gay example gone, the church would lose any psychological link to the foundations of its moral-metaphysical system, natural law, which it has held since Thomas Aquinas and the thirteenth century. Note that worries over the purported unnaturalness of masturbation and contraception just do not rile up the masses anymore; indeed, such worries simply seem silly to most people. Catholic women in America use contraceptives to the same degree that non-Catholic women do.[4] Appeals to unnatural uses of sex organs have even dropped out of public debate over abortion. That debate now turns entirely around the issue of whether abortion counts as murder or not. And no one in the pews supposes that papal views on welfare policy and labor rights have anything to do with metaphysics. If the sinfulness of homosexuality goes, so goes that which was distinctive about the *grounds* of morality for Catholicism. At least for the short term, Catholicism is a lost cause for gay progress.[5]

By contrast, mainline Protestant denominations are now gripped in titanic struggles over issues of gay connectedness. This struggle should come as no surprise given the Christian commitment to an ethics of love, an ethics that says you are not alone. Religious bars to gay connectedness put Christian churches in the conceptually awkward position of telling some people that they do not have access to what most people—and they themselves—take to be the core forms and intensities of Christianity's highest value. Struggles within mainline Protestant denominations over gay issues can be thought of as the exteriorization of this cognitive dissonance at the core of Christian thought, a dissonance caused by a clash between Levitical injunctions and revelations of love. And despite the current spate of heresy trials, excommunications, disfellowships, schisms,[6] threats of schism,[7] and the like, I expect that within ten years most mainline denominations will come around on gay issues, acknowledging that, yes, gay love is love, and recognizing, in turn, that gay love calls for social husbandry and institutional reform. The Unitarian-Universalist Association, Reform and Reconstructionist Judaism, and the United Church of Christ have already come around to this position—accepting gay clergy and performing gay holy union ceremonies and civil weddings, sometimes even to the point of civil disobedience.[8] After months of rancorous debate, the June 2003 national ratification of Gene Robinson's election as the first openly gay bishop in the Episcopal church was a watershed event in the history of American religion, especially when paired with the same national church council's formal acknowledgment that its clergy are performing same-sex wedding ceremonies.[9]

In March 2004, a "jury nullification" of church doctrine upended heresy charges pressed against a lesbian United Methodist Church minister by the church's Judicial Council, the equivalent of its Supreme Court. The United Methodist Church is the second largest Protestant denomination in America. At the "ecclesiastical trial," a jury of thirteen of the lesbian's fellow ministers refused to find her guilty of being a self-avowed, practicing homosexual, even though she told them that that was exactly what she was.[10] Dogma cannot long hold out against such forces. Love may not conquer all, but it is conquering where love is taken to be the most important of values.

*And take politicians and the judiciary themselves.* In July 2004, Senate Republicans bypassed the Senate Judiciary Committee to force a floor vote on a proposed constitutional amendment barring same-sex marriages, only to discover that in their haste they could not even muster a simple majority on a cloture motion.[11] Their forty-eight votes fell twelve short of the number needed for that and a whopping nineteen short of the votes needed to pass the amendment. Worse, some Republican senators said beforehand that solely for the sake of party unity they would vote for cloture, but would then vote against the amendment itself if it came to a final vote.[12] Altogether it was an embarrassing showing for the hard Right.

Still, the Senate's Republican leadership tried to put a good face on the defeat, claiming the vote would serve as a battle cry in upcoming elections and would rile up the populace distraught over the very thought of same-sex marriages. But even before the Senate vote, when the first unquestionably legal same sex-marriages had actually got rolling in Massachusetts two months earlier, the weddings were greeted with yawns in the pews and barrooms of America—to the consternation of leaders in the "family values" movement.[13] Unlike San Francisco's lesbian and gay weddings, which were continuously in the press through their February–March 2004 run, the Massachusetts marriages were in the papers for a day then vanished. The weekend after the start of the Massachusetts weddings on May 17, 2004, the *New York Times*' Sunday "Week in Review" section devoted only two column-inches, "Gay Rites," to a story that had been daily front-page news only five days earlier.[14] That quickly did gay marriage normalize, become an everyday event. When the sky failed to fall and the populace riot, there wasn't much to report.

The nation's judiciary will not fail to notice the collapse of the drive to amend the federal Constitution and the (perhaps surprising) absence of widespread, deep offense taken at actual, not just prospective, gay marriages. Perhaps after all it was just the prospect—the idea—of gay marriages that was scary, not real-world ones. In any case, within these political and cultural opportunities, the judiciary will find the wiggle room and interstices in which it may further pry open spaces for the advancement of lesbian and gay rights, presence, and connectedness.

There is already some evidence of a "grassroots" movement in the courts around gay marriage. In separate cases, criminal charges against a mayor and two Unitarian ministers who had "illegally" performed same-sex civil marriages were thrown out of court by New York trial judges on the grounds that the state's different-sex-only marriage law was an unconstitutional violation of equality.[15] And a circuit court in Oregon has upheld a trial judge's ruling that the state has to register the three thousand same-sex marriages conducted in Portland, Oregon, during March and April 2004, even though the judge did not believe that the state constitution required the issuance of same-sex marriage licenses and indeed barred further issuance of them.[16] The ruling was in keeping with a general trend in American family law that tries to acknowledge wherever possible couples' relationships as marriages even in the face of legal niceties to the contrary.

Meanwhile, the hard Right seems driven to increasingly desperate, even panicked, measures around same-sex marriage. In the days immediately preceding the beginning of same-sex marriages in Massachusetts, family-values operatives resorted to a "Hail Mary" pass to the federal judiciary. They tried to enlist the federal courts to block the marriages from happening by getting the courts to declare that the Massachusetts supreme court's same-sex marriage rulings violated the federal Constitution's obscure and all but forgotten Guarantee Clause, by which the federal government has an obligation to guarantee that the states have republican—that's small-r "republican"—forms of government. The Right's argument was that what four Massachusetts judges had done was so crazy that they had de facto turned Massachusetts into a monarchy with themselves as its kings and queens. The unprecedented argument went nowhere. The federal district court refused to grant a temporary injunction stopping the marriages. On a quick appeal, the federal circuit court did the same, though it said it would eventually hear the case on its merits. And the Supreme Court, without even one recorded dissent, declined to get involved. When the circuit court eventually heard the argument on its merits, it found none.[17]

Once the Federal Marriage Amendment failed in the Senate, Republicans in the House attempted an end run around the Constitution. They began efforts to pass a federal law that would prohibit the federal courts, including the Supreme Court, from hearing cases on the constitutionality of the Defense of Marriage Act (1996), which prohibits the federal government and insulates state governments from acknowledging same-sex marriages.[18] Especially after the Supreme Court's 2004 right-asserting, Right-denying terrorism cases, it seems hopelessly unlikely that the federal courts are going to say that another branch of government can totally shut down the courts' jurisdiction in a given area by claiming that some group has no rights that the courts can apply on its behalf.[19] More specifically, the proposed legislation also seems to forget *Romer v. Evans* and its promise to lesbians and gay men that government "cannot deem a class of persons a stranger to its law"—all the more so when the law in question is the fundamental law of the land.[20]

When the Right is not panicking, it is providing surprising and striking examples of shifts on gay family issues. Consider again Sen. Trent Lott. In 1998, he was comparing gay men and lesbians to child molesters, sex addicts, kleptomaniacs, and alcoholics.[21] In June 2004, during the same *New York Times Magazine* interview in which he held that the U.S. military's abuse of prisoners in Iraq was perfectly all right by his lights, he claimed that it was also fine with him if gay men jointly adopt and raise children and are treated legally as families: "It's so important that children have parents or family that love them. There are a lot of adopted children who have loving parents, and it comes in different ways with different people in different states."[22] Call him Mister Diversity.

Even President Bush shifted. As the governor of Texas, he had defended in the courts the state's sexual-orientation-specific sodomy law by appealing to the purported educational value of the law for the state's young people. But after his state's sodomy law had been declared unconstitutional in *Lawrence v. Texas*, he redrew his line in the sand.[23] In the days leading up to the failed Senate vote on the Federal Marriage Amendment, he thought that same-sex sodomy was fine, indeed all-American, only just not same-sex marriage. He still managed, though, to do all this without actually naming gay people: "What they do in the privacy of their house, consenting adults should be able to do. This is America. It's a free society. But it doesn't mean we have to redefine traditional marriage."[24] Bush's shift and the resulting instability of this jumble of thoughts holds great promise.

* * *

And this progress is occurring because the culture itself is changing. The pictures of lesbian and gay newlyweds beaming their love from the steps of San Francisco City Hall and the weddings pages of the *New York Times* turn not just heads, but hearts. Consistent political progress will be made only when those committed to justice change the general cognitive atmosphere and the effective feelings of the "common man," constituted and driven as they are by stereotypes, bogeys, and vestiges of taboo. The needed change will occur not by accommodating these feelings or pandering to populism, but by changing the culture that bears and nurtures them. Change the culture and political forms will, in general and in the long run, follow suit. And the strength of cultural forces should not be underestimated. It was blue jeans and video cassettes that won the Cold War for the West—not hydrogen bombs and uranium-clad tanks.

Now, the good news is that lesbians, gay men, and our allies have or are rapidly coming to have creative access to the machinery of cultural change—the media, even media empires, the arts, books, magazines, editorial pages, educational forums, talk shows, movies, plays, computer networks, religious study groups, employee groups, and the like. To a large degree, hope for a better lesbian and gay future lies along these vectors of transformation rather than in poster-paint and cardboard.

When gay men and lesbians do choose to invest in politics narrowly understood, strategies should be chosen with an eye to their effect in transforming culture rather than specifically as means of garnering votes. Political participation itself is a cultural form that, if played out correctly, can have positive cultural consequences even in the face of electoral failure. Note that a placard which reads "No on 2: Stop Discrimination" or "Maine Won't Discriminate" does no educating, changes no culture. Indeed it leaves gay issues entirely unmentioned, just exactly the way antigay forces want them. By contrast, placards which read, "I'm gay," or "My son is gay," or "Straights for Gay Rights" both educate and change culture.

And they change culture in part because their message has a tug on people's feelings, on the way people view things. Remember how stereotypes work: they are not (simply) false inductions from skewed samples, something that science could fix; rather they operate as mental lenses through which people perceive, evaluate, even construct the world, and so they tend to be self-perpetuating, for they cause people to notice only things that support what they already believe. In consequence, education, to be effective, cannot simply be an attempt to get the facts right— that effort is too easily derailed by the very stereotypes that "diversity" education is trying to dispel. To sloganize: America treats gays badly not because it has the wrong facts but because it has the wrong ideas.

Taking a cultural view of politics helps sort out some of the currently tangled gay political scene. It means, for instance, that the current disarray of national gay and lesbian political organizations and especially the waning of traditional activist forms and of grassroots politicking may not be the disasters that they at first appear to be—if, that is, the general culture is moving in the right direction. Take Canada. There gays can serve openly in the armed forces, have been given the highest level of constitutional protections, have legislated civil rights protections in all provinces, have common law marital privileges right across the country, and access to full formal civil marriages in Ontario, British Columbia, Quebec, and the Yukon.[25] These gains have been achieved even though the country had no national gay political organization until 1986, and that organization, Egale, now has only three thousand members. Things stand similarly for gay-progressive Norway. It's the culture that counts.

More important for change now than gay political groups (whether national or grassroots) are *culturally* engaged but locally or topically focused groups, groups like Parents and Friends of Lesbians and Gays, gay academic, religious, and labor caucuses, antidefamation groups (like the Gay and Lesbian Alliance against Defamation [GLAAD]), Men of All Colors Together, the Gay, Lesbian, and Straight Educational

Network, indeed any group that is open and pointed about working for gay and lesbian issues. What I'm suggesting is that if a sewing circle has a letter-writing potluck, it would be wise to write letters to the local television station and to CBS as well as to the mayor and senators. Those working for gays' justice need to make active outreach efforts to libraries, school boards, PTAs, religious roundtables, trade union coalitions, chambers of commerce, Elk, Moose, Eagle, Rotarian, and Odd Fellow Clubs—and wherever it is that judges hang out.

In this broad culturally oriented view of lesbian and gay politics, much that one might not at first think of as political actually is so. Activist leaders have bemoaned the fact that current lesbian and gay youth, though leading open lives, are most often apolitical. But these brave youth are key to culture's change on lesbian and gay men's issues. Thanks to them, increasingly people know someone for whom being gay is an issue. Thanks to them the lesbian and gay movement is achieving critical mass. When lesbians and gay men come out, what matters in political debates is drawn from the spectral world of fear and symbolism into, well, the neighborhood.

And some gay critics have rued the fact that virtually all the mainstream media coverage of lesbian and gay events, though sometimes extensive, is "soft news": personality profiles and entertainment coverage galore, yet nothing political, nothing about gay rights. But "soft news" changes culture. A newspaper feature in "Lifestyles" about a lesbian couple who run a real estate business is at least as culturally important as a gay pride parade pictured on page 1. The parade is the extraordinary. The lesbians are America's neighbors. To acknowledge their everydayness is to change the everyday.

\* \* \*

Now suppose—fantasize for a second—that down the road a decade or two or three, justice for gays and lesbians is fully achieved in the legal realm—all the laws are fixed. What, if anything, would then remain for the gay movement to achieve?

Even the most casual observation of the status of blacks in America after the Civil Rights era suggests that even after legal justice is achieved

for gays, lots will likely remain to be done socially and culturally. There
are currently no race-specific national laws that black America is pressing for passage. The legislative agenda for blacks, as far as anyone can
tell, is complete. With the Supreme Court's acceptance, in 2003, of
racially keyed affirmative action programs in education, the judicial
agenda for blacks too is largely complete.[26] Yet, socially and culturally,
blacks are hardly equal in America. Schools are now more segregated
by race in America than they were when *Brown v. the Board of Education*
was announced in 1954.[27] Northern cities, like Chicago, are more
racially segregated than rural southern towns. Despite the reformation
in black legal equality, white America has not let black America assimilate into mainstream culture. With respect to blacks, America has rejected not only a "melting pot" model of race relations, but even a "stir
fry" model, in which distinctive modes of ethnicity are retained, if altered, as they are mixed together to the advantage of both the parts and
the whole. Whites have voted with their feet and checkbooks to maintain the dominant culture as white culture. The few well-placed blacks
in America, whether on the golf course or Supreme Court, operate like
the single candle in Kafka's cathedral. Its light makes the darkness
darker. They turn white a lighter shade of pale.

How things fare for lesbians and gays *after legal justice is achieved*
will depend on whether America lets gays and lesbians assimilate into
mainstream culture—or rather, whether America undergoes a dialectical development between mainstream culture and gay and lesbian experience that incorporates ordinary, openly gay folk into the national
jambalaya. An ideal American television series, for instance, would
take ordinary gay and lesbian folk for granted, as a given foreground
presence in social and familial landscapes, but also would have gays'
and lesbians' distinctive experience make a difference to how the series' programs unfold. Just about the only piece of popular culture that
I can think of to date that has clearly met this standard is practically an
antiquity now: Rainer Werner Fassbinder's 1975 film *Fox and His
Friends*. The movie has ordinary gay men as its lead characters, but it
is not about being gay, even ordinarily gay; it's about love, money,
gullibility, and trust, but how these themes play out turns on the distinctive life ways of the gay characters. Perhaps Alan Ball's television

series for HBO *Six Feet Under* and Jonathan Caouette's 2003 art documentary *Tarnation* meet this standard as well.

There is some reason to think that America *will* add gay men and lesbians to the country's conglomeration. The trajectory of gays in America, after legal justice, will probably be more like that of Jews after the Civil Rights era than that of blacks. Jews were both a major constituency and major force in getting the 1964 Civil Rights Act passed. At the time, it was thought that Jews would be major beneficiaries of its provisions, but in fact there are almost no Civil Rights Act cases with Jewish plaintiffs.[28] Blatant discrimination against Jews trailed off just as legal protections against such discrimination were coming into play. Discrimination against Jews now tends to be too sinuous and fine grained to trigger or easily be addressed by either the "smoking gun" or "disparate impact" analyses that are the nuts and bolts of lawsuits under the 1964 Civil Rights Act.

Jews were allowed to assimilate because Jews were emblematic of the modern. If Andrew Hacker is right, blacks have not been allowed to assimilate because the dominant culture takes blacks as emblematic of the primitive.[29] As emblems of the modern (and even of the postmodern), gays and Jews are fraternal twins. Try to think of the Manhattan or Los Angeles catchments without them. One can't.

And gays and lesbians have another leg up in the process of national inclusion. We were virtually all raised in straight families, and when we get our families to cease feeling embarrassed about us and begin treating us as the loved and loving, helpsome and winning folk they know us to be, then the constituency for the wider political, social, and cultural acceptance of gays suddenly becomes a force to be reckoned with.

\* \* \*

I expect, though, that one form of cultural resistance to the social acceptance of gay men and lesbians will be as long lasting as it is uniquely insidious. It is what I want to call "the heterosexual presumption." American culture, even as it now talks about gays—and so presumably believes that gays exist somewhere—can simultaneously operate upon a presumption that everyone is heterosexual. It is certainly capable of speaking that way.

American love songs presume that all sexuality is heterosexuality and often assume that this universality is underwritten by the cosmos itself. Thus Americans ritualize the passage of time and sing in the New Year with the lyrics, "Woman needs man / And man must have his mate / That no one can deny ... . / The fundamental things apply / As time goes by."[30] This is an easy case. There are more complicated, tangled ones. Unlike the author of "As Time Goes By," the teller of fag jokes necessarily knows that gays exist—why tell jokes about creatures who don't—but the teller *speaks* both as though there are no gays in his audience and as though he speaks for and to "everyman." Everyone is his presumed coconspirator, a sharer in the values that engine the joke's belittling fun. So at the same time and in the same respect, gays both do and do not exist. Philosophers call that a contradiction.

*Newsweek* magazine has managed to cast this contradiction into explicit, if still unacknowledged, form. Consider an astonishing cheek-to-jowl juxtaposition of a detailed knowledge of gays and an ability to assume that everyone is straight. It is the lead for an article on gay couples in the magazine's June 25, 2003, issue: "Yes, gay men are having more sex than you are. But if it makes you feel any better, lesbians are probably not." The article presumes that its entire potential audience—"you," Americans—has in it not one gay man or lesbian, even as the subject of the article is the lives of gay and lesbian Americans.

Or again: Dockside news reports of soldiers and sailors shipping out to and returning from the Middle East presume that all the people coming and going are heterosexual, that is, are people who are expected in their comings and goings to hug and smooch their girlfriends, boyfriends, and spouses in public with gusto.[31] What does the American press think lesbian and gay couples with military members do on these docks? Mainstream advice columns—"Ten Ways to Catch a Guy," "What Not to Give Her on Valentine's Day," and dozens of other msn.com home page links—all presume that all people are heterosexual. Ninety-nine and forty-four one-hundredths percent of references to "having children" do the same. And of course parents presume their children are straight; after all, their children are people.

The heterosexual presumption is the culture's default position. The presumption does not govern thought the way an axiom governs thought in a mathematical proof, acting as an explicit, articulated premise. Rather it is an unarticulated background condition. It does not draw attention to itself, but is as pervasive as it is unobtrusive. It operates like air at room temperature or like a computer's software. People are not aware of it, though it conditions everything they do.

What does get noticed and articulated by culture is any sudden, unusual departure from the bland background. But just as quickly as such dislocations appear, they are reabsorbed into the presumption's fog, fall back below the cultural radar. The culture will speak of gays when there is a particular reason for attention to be drawn to them (say, in a news story, a court case, a gay-themed television program), but then slides back into the normal run of things and presumes again that everyone is straight—without ever having to articulate that this is what it is doing. A person in one breath will say, "Well, some of my best friends are gay," while singing "As Time Goes By" with the next.

Other groups are subject to a similar presumption. If I use the gender and race-neutral term "president," the image that probably springs to your mind is that of a white male, even if you are not a white male. Hardly anyone who is in the position to have the thought "Gosh, everyone on this airplane is white" ever does have it. And classically, English can use "mankind" to refer to both men and women even though it names only men.

The lines laid out by such cultural presumptions plat what is to count as a person worth acknowledging, a person of relevance, a member of the moral community, one who belongs. The relevant analogy for the relation between the culturally presumed person and the irrelevant person is not the relation of a human to something viewed as having a lower moral standing than humans have, say, children, worms, fungus, excrement, the abject. Rather here the relevant analogy is the relation of citizen to alien. Gays are America's "internal aliens." America thinks of gays the way it thinks of Canadians, which is to say, as wholly forgettable. It is not that Americans don't think Canadians are people, it's just that Americans have arranged their thoughts so they don't have occasion to take cognizance of Canadians, except if something peculiar comes up that draws special attention to them (say, the sudden availability of full marriage for gays in Ontario). For Americans, the concept "North American" has no cultural content. What could have a thick content and denote important relations between diverse social types (Americans, Canadians, and others) is at best for Americans a geographic concept that they heard about for the last time in eighth grade. And it goes without saying that Americans don't think Canadians' interests count on a par with their own, and in a way they shouldn't, because they are there, not here. They have their own national interest, as do Americans. But gays *are* here. And so it appears we need to keep chanting the Queer Nation slogan, "We're here, we're queer, get used to it." But the slogan needs a suffix: " ... get used to it, and don't forget it."

As the *Newsweek* example shows, culture can, without change or acknowledgement, absorb mountains of cognitive dissonance and contradiction: "Gays exist in the population, but no one of us is ever one of them." Race and gender examples show that such presumptions are deeply entrenched. As an invisible minority, gays are at an enormous disadvantage compared to visible minorities in trying to overcome the presumption that erases their existence even as it speaks of it. Gays and lesbians come "preerased," erased to appearance to begin with.

Being out is one means of nibbling away at the heterosexual presumption. Though when one challenges the presumption, the presumption itself prompts and falsely justifies the too-facile charge that one is "flaunting it." The presumption makes any "standing out" look like "acting out." Resistance in these circumstances is endlessly exhausting. This interpenetration of resistance and exhaustion, which usually occurs at the microlevel of social interactions, helps explain a significant part of the constant, diffuse uneasiness that gay men and lesbians feel in society, like having a low grade fever that you just can't shake.

Caricatures of heterosexuality are probably an even more effective means of addressing "the presumption," since parody makes a theme of the very issue in question—as in the last two lines of Billy Wilder's *Some Like It Hot* (1959). When Jack Lemmon, in drag, responds to Joe E. Brown's marriage proposal with the line, "You don't understand, I'm a man," Brown closes the show with "Nobody's perfect." Movies like Tim

Burton's *Pee-Wee's Big Adventure* (1985) and Joel Coen's *Raising Arizona* (1987) manage to demythologize heterosexuality and attack its unacknowledged embeddedness without introducing any homosexual characters. I wonder whether there are additional ways to do this. Certainly additional ways are needed. Lesbians and gay men can use all the resources we can muster for addressing this problem, one that will probably still be with us even after gays are marrying in Utah.

\* \* \*

That America views gay men and lesbians as "internal aliens" was brought home to me during the early years of lesbian and gay participation in my hometown's Fourth of July parades. Back then, knots of fraternity boys, good ol' boys, and generic hooligans would throw cans of beer and firecrackers at the heads of folk in the lesbian and gay contingent. Our ears would ring for hours after parade's end. But scarier than all that were the throngs gathered around the judging stand who, as the lesbian and gay contingent passed, would chant and stomp in unison, "Go home, go home, go home. Fags, go home." This rhythmic chanting was the phobic counterpart to the racist chant of the 1950s and beyond, "Niggers, back to Africa!" But in our case, I wondered where the crowd thought home was. After a few years of such unpleasantness, the police started citing open-container violations, and those in the crowd who were not cheering the contingent started to fall temporarily silent as it passed by them. That too felt eerie, as though the contingent were a hearse. But it also felt powerful. The silent treatment, in this case, could hardly be a shaming ritual, an enactment of "don't ask, don't tell." For there we were, telling about us like crazy— and, in a way, telling on them too. They were forced to think about themselves for once. This reversed silencing may be a sign that the heterosexual presumption has its fissures, and so perhaps too that some progress is being made even on this front.

On all other fronts, gay men and lesbians are clearly making good, sometimes swimmingly good, progress—through the opportunities the collapse of the taboo has afforded, through lesbian and gay people telling our stories, through images that flash across television screens, movie screens, and the American mind, through family members coming out, through love.

Will Rogers correctly recognized the limited role of reason in politics when he quipped, "People's minds are changed through observation, not through argument." Certainly arguing Bible passages with fundamentalists has no point or prospect. But I think Will Rogers was wrong when he also claimed, "We do more talking progress than we do progressing." Though virtually everything remains to be done, on gay issues at least, America is gradually taking the talking cure.

# Notes

*Introduction. A Taboo's End*

1. *New York Times*, February 25, 2004, p. 1. All references are to the national edition.

2. *"The New York Times," Advocate*, February 20, 1996, p. 16.

3. *New York Times*, August 3, 2003, section 9, p. 10; February 22, 2004, section 9, p. 12.

4. *Washington Post*, July 23, 2003, p. C8.

5. *New York Times*, June 17, 1998, p. 23; June 30, 1998, p. 1.

6. "Call Off the War on Gays," *U.S. News & World Report*, August 3, 1998, p. 64.

7. *New York Times*, February 12, 1995, p. 32; March 8, 1995, p. 12; April 4, 1995, section 4, p. 23.

8. *New York Times*, February 10, 2004, section 3, p. 10.

9. *New York Times*, February 28, 1995, section 2, p. 2.

10. *Lawrence v. Texas*, 539 U.S. 558 (2003).

11. *Dale v. Boy Scouts of America*, 530 U.S. 640 (2000).

12. "Companies Cut Funding for Boy Scouts," *Wall Street Journal*, August 24, 2000; "Boy Scout Troops Lose Funds," *USA Today*, October 10, 2000.

13. *Bowers v. Hardwick*, 478 U.S. 186 (1986).

14. *Brown v. Board of Education*, 347 U.S. 483 (1954); *Plessy v. Ferguson*, 153 U.S. 537 (1896).

15. *Lofton v. Sec'y of Dept. of Children & Family Serv., Florida*, 358 F.3d 804 (2004); *State v. Limon*, 83 P.3d 229 (Kans. 2004).

16. *Goodridge v. Dept. of Public Health*, 798 N.E.2d 941 (Mass. 2003).

17. *Palmore v. Sidoti*, 466 U.S. 429 (1984) (blacks); *Craig v. Boren*, 429 U.S. 190 (1976) (women); *Plyler v. Doe*, 457 U.S. 202 (1982) (illegal immigrant children).

18. *Halpern v. Toronto*, 172 O.A.C. 276 (2003).

19. *New York Times*, September 17, 2003, p. 5.

*1. Lesbian and Gay Basics*

1. *Newsweek*, August 12, 1985, p. 23 (Gallup Poll).

2. *Washington Post*, March 8, 2004 (*Washington Post*–ABC Poll); *Los Angeles Times*, April 10, 2004 (*Los Angeles Times* Poll).

3. Evelyn Hooker, "The Adjustment of the Male Overt Homosexual," *Journal of Projective Techniques* 21 (1957): 18–31.

4. American Psychiatric Association, *Diagnostic and Statistical Manual of Mental Disorders—Fourth Edition (DSM–IV)* (Washington, D.C. American Psychiatric Association, 1994).

5. *New York Times*, February 23, 2004, p. 14.

6. Ibid.

7. *New York Times*, January 10, 2000, p. 11.

8. *Washington Post*, May 15, 1984, p. 1.

9. *New York Times*, November 5, 1999, p. 1.

10. *New York Times*, November 2, 1999, p. 14.

11. "Rapper's Hate-Filled Lyrics Anger Some," *USA Today*, July 27, 2000.

12. "1,049 Laws Benefit Married Couples, GAO Says," *Washington Blade*, February 21, 1997.

13. *New York Times*, December 12, 1993, p. 19.

14. *Lawrence v. Texas*, 539 U.S. 558 (2003).

15. John Boswell, *Christianity, Social Tolerance, and Homosexuality* (Chicago: University of Chicago Press, 1980), chapter 4.

16. Gilbert Herdt, *Guardians of the Flute* (New York: McGraw-Hill, 1981).

17. Leviticus 18:22, 21:3 (condemnations of same-sex sex acts); Leviticus 11:1–47, 15:19–27 (dietary and hygienic codes); Genesis 19:1–25 (Lot at Sodom), 19:30–38 (Lot in cave).

18. See generally, Robert P. George, editor, *Natural Law Theory: Contemporary Essays* (Oxford: Oxford University Press, 1992).

19. *New York Times*, April 1, 2004, p. 1.

20. Hannah Arendt, *The Human Condition* (Chicago: University of Chicago Press, 1958), chapter 1.

21. See Edward Stein, *The Mismeasure of Desire* (New York: Oxford University Press, 2001).

22. See Claudia Card, *Lesbian Choices* (New York: Columbia University Press, 1995); Cheshire Calhoun, *Feminism, the Family, and the Politics of the Closet* (Oxford: Oxford University Press, 2000).

23. *Cleveland Plain Dealer*, November 11, 1999, p. 1B.

24. *Baker v. State*, 170 Vt. 194; 744 A.2d 864 (1999); *New York Times*, December 28, 1999, p. 18.

25. *New York Times*, September 14, 2001, p. 13.

26. *New York Times*, December 20, 2000, p. 6.

27. *New York Times*, June 10, 2000, p. 6.

28. *New York Times*, March 20, 2004, p. 5.

29. *New York Times*, June 22, 2004, p. 5.

30. *New York Times*, December 7, 2002, p. 8; "Britain Proposes 'Gay Marriage' Plan," Irish Examiner.com, April 1, 2004, www.examiner.ie/pport/web/Full_Story/did-sgFJqm3hrTI3csgoaewFBADppk.asp (accessed June 22, 2004).

31. *Goodridge v. Dept. of Public Health*, 798 N.E.2d 941 (Mass. 2003); *In re Opinions of the Justices to the Senate*, 802 N.E.2d 565 (Mass. 2004).

32. *New York Times*, May 23, 2004, section 4, p. 2.

33. *New York Times*, September 26, 2000, section 3, p. 2.

34. *New York Times*, February 29, 2004, section 2, p. 1.

35. *Morning Edition*, National Public Radio, June 30, 2004.

36. *New York Times*, March 18, 2004, p. 21; *Champaign (Ill.) News Gazette*, Associated Press wire story (San Francisco), March 18, 2004, p. E1.

37. *New York Times*, April 21, 2004, p. 19.

38. "Reagan Appoints Antigay Judge to Supreme Court," *Lesbian/Gay Law Notes* (December 1987): 69.

39. *Society for Individual Rights v. Hampton*, 528 F.2d 905 (1975) (federal employment); *Singer v. U.S. Civil Service Commission*, 530 F.2d 247 (1976) (federal employment); *Beller v. Middendorf*, 632 F.2d 788 (1980) (upholding ban on gays in the military); *Sullivan v. Immigration and Naturalization Service*, 772 F.2d 609 (1985) (holding that gay relationships do not count for possible hardship exceptions to INS deportation orders).

*2. Sexual Privacy*

1. *Lawrence v. Texas*, 539 U.S. 558 (2003); Bowers v. Hardwick, 478 U.S. 186 (1986).

2. For a detailed analysis of these lines and of the confusions of the *Lawrence* decision more generally, see Richard D. Mohr, "The Shag-a-delic Supreme Court: 'Anal Sex,' 'Mystery,' 'Destiny,' and the 'Transcendent' in *Lawrence v. Texas*," *Cardozo Women's Law Journal* 10 (2004): 365–95.

3. *New York Times*, July 6, 2003, section 4, p. 3.

4. *Dallas Morning News*, June 27, 2003, p. 19.

5. See L. C. Becker, *Property Rights: Philosophical Foundations* (New York: Routledge, 1977), chapter 4.

6. *Planned Parenthood v. Casey*, 505 U.S. 833 (1992).

7. *New York Times*, July 30, 2003, p. 12; August 9, 2003, p. 10.

8. Larry Kramer, "AIDS: We Asked for It," *Advocate*, May 27, 1997, p. 59.

9. "Bathhouses in the Balance," *San Diego City Beat*, June 19, 2004.

10. See classically, Ronald Dworkin, *Taking Rights Seriously* (Cambridge, Mass.: Harvard University Press, 1977), chapters 4–7.

11. See classically, John Stuart Mill, *On Liberty* (1859), chapter 1.

12. *Goodridge v. Dept. of Public Health*, 798 N.E.2d 941 (Mass. 2003).

*3. The Case for Lesbian and Gay Marriage*

1. *Michael M. v. Sonoma County*, 450 U.S. 464 (1981).

2. *Lawrence v. Texas*, 539 U.S. 558 (2003).

3. *New York Times*, March 19, 2004, p. 13.

4. Harry D. Krause and David D. Meyer, *Family Law: In a Nutshell*, 5th edition (St. Paul, Minn.: West, 2005).

5. *Washington Post*, May 2, 2003, p. 1.

6. *New York Times Magazine*, November 27, 1994, pp. 54–55.

7. *Washington Post*, May 2, 2003, p. 1.

8. Leslie J. Harris, "Marriage," *Oxford Companion to American Law*, Kermit Hall, editor (New York: Oxford University Press, 2002).

9. Philip Blumstein and Pepper Schwartz, *American Couples* (New York: Morrow, 1983); David McWhirter and Andrew Mattison, *The Male Couple* (Englewood Cliffs, N.J.: Prentice-Hall, 1984); Kath Weston, *Families We Choose* (New York: Columbia University Press, 1991); Christopher Carrington, *No Place Like Home* (Chicago: University of Chicago Press, 2002).

10. Claudia Card, *Lesbian Choices* (New York: Columbia University Press, 1995), chapters 3–6.

11. *Weber v. Aetna Cas. & Sur. Co.*, 406 U.S. 164 (1972).

12. *Moore v. City of East Cleveland*, 431 U.S. 494 (1977).

## 4. Equality

1. *Dred Scott v. Sandford*, 60 U.S. 393 (1856).

2. *Dept. of Agriculture v. Moreno*, 413 U.S. 528 (1973).

3. Congregation for the Doctrine of the Faith, "Declaration Persona Humana" (December 29, 1975); "Letter on the Pastoral Care of Homosexual Persons" (October 1, 1986); "Some Considerations Concerning the Response to Legislative Proposals on the Non-discrimination of Homosexual Persons (July 24, 1992); "Considerations Regarding Proposals to Give Legal Recognition to Unions between Homosexual Persons" (July 31, 2003).

4. Randy Shilts, *And the Band Played On* (New York: St. Martin's, 1987), p. 554.

5. Hans Peter Bleuel, *Strength and Joy: Sex and Society in Nazi Germany* (London: Secker and Warburg, 1973), p. 221.

6. *United States v. Carolene Products Co.*, 304 U.S. 144 (1938) (religious groups); *Palmore v. Sidoti*, 466 U.S. 429 (1984) (ethnic and racial groups); *Graham v. Richardson*, 403 U.S. 365 (1971) (legal aliens); *Plyler v. Doe*, 457 U.S. 202 (1982) (illegal immigrant children), *Weber v. Aetna Cas. & Sur. Co.*, 406 U.S. 164 (1972) (illegitimate children); Craig v. Boren, 429 U.S. 190 (1976) (women); *Cleburne v. Cleburne Living Center, Inc.*, 473 U.S. 432 (1985) (mentally and physically challenged).

7. *Plessy v. Ferguson*, 163 U.S. 537 (1896).

8. *Loving v. Virginia*, 388 U.S. 1 (1967).

9. *Goodridge v. Dept. of Public Health*, 798 N.E.2d 941 (Mass. 2003); *In re Opinions of the Justices to the Senate*, 802 N.E.2d 565 (Mass. 2004).

## 5. Civil Rights

1. *Dale v. Boy Scouts of America*, 530 U.S. 640 (2000).

2. *Romer v. Evans*, 517 U.S. 620 (1996).

3. Alfred Kinsey et al., *Sexual Behavior in the Human Male* (Philadelphia: Saunders, 1948), see also M. V. Lee Badgett, *Money, Myths, and Change: The Economic Lives of Lesbians and Gay Men* (Chicago: University of Chicago Press, 2001).

4. "Out and Elected Officials," www.victoryinstitute.org (accessed April 11, 2004); *New York Times*, August 15, 2004, section 4, p. 1.

5. *Lawrence v. Texas*, 539 U.S. 558 (2003); Romer v. Evans, 517 U.S. 620 (1996).

6. Department of Defense Directive 1332.14, *Federal Register*, January 29, 1981, 46(19):9571–78.

7. *In re Opinions of the Justices to the Senate*, 802 N.E.2d 565 (Mass. 2004).

8. United Press International wire story, Tallahassee, Fla., August 30, 1996.

9. *New York Times*, April 22, 1995, p. 6.

10. *New York Times*, February 24, 2004, p. 1.

11. *Palmore v. Sidoti*, 466 U.S. 429 (1984).

*6. Understanding Lesbians and Gay Men in the Military*

1. See 10 U.S.C.A. § 654 (1995).

2. *New York Times*, March 24, 2004, p. 14.

3. "Public OK with Gays, Women in Military," Gallup Organization, December 23, 2003, www.gallup.com (accessed April 16, 2004).

4. *New York Times*, January 13, 2000, p. 1.

5. *New York Times*, November 15, 2002, p. 18.

6. *Policy Concerning Homosexuality in the Armed Forces: Hearings before the Committee on Armed Services*, U.S. Senate, 103rd Congress, 2nd session, March 29, 31; April 29; May 7, 10, 11; July 20, 21, 22, 1993; Senate Hearing 103-845, p. 597.

7. "For Gays, Secrecy in Love, War," *Los Angeles Times*, April 16, 2003; "Lesbian Baiting, Statistics through FY 2000," Servicemembers Legal Defense Network, www.sldn.org (accessed April 11, 2004).

8. *New York Times*, March 16, 2003, p. 1.

9. James D. Steakley, *The Homosexual Emancipation Movement in Germany* (New York: Arno, 1975), p. 111.

10. See, for images, *New York Times*, April 21, 2004, p. 1; May 23, 2004, p. 1.

11. A splendid example can be seen on permanent display at the J. Paul Getty Museum, Brentwood, Los Angeles—"Grave Stele of Pollis," unknown artist, Megara, c. 480 B.C., 60 1/4" high, accession number 90.AA.129—or at the Getty Web site www.getty.edu/art/collections/objects/015195.html (accessed April 16, 2004).

*Conclusion. America's Promise and the Lesbian and Gay Future*

1. Alexis de Tocqueville, *The Old Regime and the Revolution* (1856).

2. *New York Times*, March 16, 2004, p. 21.

3. See classically, Eve Sedgwick, *The Epistemology of the Closet* (Berkeley: University of California Press, 1990), introduction and chapter 1.

4. *New York Times*, November 13, 2003, p. 16.

5. For a more sympathetic reading of Catholic doctrine, though still from a liberal perspective, see Andrew Koppelman, *The Gay Rights Question in*

*Contemporary American Law* (Chicago: University of Chicago Press, 2002), chapter 4.

6. *New York Times*, June 16, 2004, p. 14 (Southern Baptists from World Baptist Alliance).

7. *New York Times*, July 24, 2003, p. 12 (conservative Anglicans from Episcopal Church USA); *New York Times*, May 7, 2004, p. 16 (conservative Methodists from United Methodist Church).

8. *New York Times*, January 30, 2004, p. 1; March 16, 2004, p. 21.

9. *New York Times*, August 6, 2003, p. 1; August 8, 2003, p. 10.

10. *New York Times*, March 22, 2004, p. 16.

11. *New York Times*, July 15, 2004, p. 1

12. Ibid.

13. *Washington Post*, June 19, 2004, p. A3.

14. *New York Times*, May 23, 2004, section 4, p. 2.

15. "Judge Clears West, Says State Wrong to Block Gay Marriages," *Kingston (N.Y.) Daily Freeman*, June 11, 2004; "Judge Dismisses Charges against Ministers Who Married Gay Couples," *Sarasota (Fla.) Herald-Tribune* (AP wire story, Albany, N.Y.), July 13, 2004.

16. "Court Orders Oregon to Record Same-Sex Marriages," *Salem (Ore.) Statesman Journal* (AP wire story), July 9, 2004.

17. *Largess v. Supreme Judicial Court of Massachusetts*, 373 F.3d 219 (2004).

18. *New York Times*, July 15, 2004, p. 1.

19. *Rasul v. Bush*, 124 S.Ct. 2686 (2004); *Hamdi v. Rumsfeld*, 124 S.Ct. 2633 (2004).

20. *Romer v. Evans*, 517 U.S. 620 (1996).

21. *New York Times*, June 30, 1998, p. 1.

22. *New York Times Magazine*, June 20, 2004, p. 15.

23. *Lawrence v. Texas*, 539 U.S. 558 (2003).

24. *New York Times*, July 10, 2004, p. 14.

25. *New York Times*, July 22, 2004, p. 4.

26. *Grutter v. Bollinger*, 539 U.S. 244 (2003).

27. *Brown v. Board of Education*, 347 U.S. 483 (1954).

28. See Paul Burstein, *Discrimination, Jobs, and Politics* (Chicago: University of Chicago, 1985).

29. Andrew Hacker, *Two Nations: Black and White, Separate, Hostile, Unequal* (New York: Scribner's, 1992).

30. Herman Hupfeld (1894–1951), "As Time Goes By" (New York: Harms, 1931).

31. *New York Times*, April 18, 2003, section 2, p. 9.

# Acknowledgments

I thank the many people who helped conceive the book as a project and who helped realize the project as a book: the late James Rachels, Claudia Mills, Deborah Chasman, Brad Hebel, Suzanne Ryan, John Littlewood, Rex Wockner, Andrew Koppelman, Simon D. Stern, and Robert W. Switzer.